Crime Scene Investigation: CSI

The Unauthorized Guide to the CBS Hit show
CSI Las Vegas: Season Two

By: Kristina Benson

The Unauthorized Guide to the CBS Hit Show CSI Las Vegas: Season Two

ISBN: 978-1-60332-026-9

Edited By: Brooke Winger

Printed in the United States of America

Table of Contents

Episode Guide

Episode One: Burked

A gardener arrives at a beautiful home in Las Vegas and is greeted by two happy yellow labs as he gets out of his truck. He wanders through the lush greenery surrounding the home and peers through the blinds. There is a body on the floor.

The next shot is of Gil and Catherine arriving on the scene to walk towards the body. Catherine, in this scene, fills the function of providing exposition, telling us that the house belongs to Tony Braun, son of Vegas business mogul Sam Braun. She explains that he came to Vegas to revitalize it when it looked like its peak had come and gone. He allegedly had ties to Bugsy Siegel.

Brass arrives and they all proceed to examine the body. An empty pill bottle and crushed foil indicates that he had been popping pills and taking heroin while lying around the house in his underwear. The credits roll.

When we come back from break, Sara is taking photos. She pauses, staring at the shag carpet for a moment before picking up a pair of tweezers and extracting an earring.

Grissom then observes Tony has adhesive on his wrists.
The two of them conclude that Tony had company that
evening. They then wonder if that someone had cleaned up
the body: usually a dead body voids itself of fluids rather
rapidly, and at this scene, there are none present. Sara
points at Tony's torso, noting three small red marks, and
comments, "Interesting love bites on his chest." She also
notes that the body is posed. She asks Gil when he figured
this to be a homicide instead of a drug overdose, and Gil
replies, "When I saw the TV on."

Outside, Catherine is judging people who have heroin
addictions and gathering clues from the outside of the
house. The gardener had said that this one morning was
the first time in five years the gate had been left open, and
that there is no sign of forced entry.

Warrick appears, goes inside, and looks at the buffet of
drug paraphernalia littering the top of a dresser. "A heroin
addict's confetti. Must have been going on a binge," he
says. He picks up a balloon and observes that the inside is
filled with black tar heroin. Brass comes in and asks
Warrick if he can get a print of those balloons; Warrick
turns around and says with a swagger, "I can get a print off
of air."

Down in the kitchen, Sara is pawing through the garbage and finds a box of saltines with duct tape inside.

Later, at the morgue, Gil walks in on David the coroner examining the sole of his shoe. When he sees Grissom, he ceases and desists doing so and gives us a lowdown on the body. "His lifestyle was no secret -- sex, drugs and a big bankroll. Whatever he did went up his nose; his nasal cavity looked like raw hamburger." Gil observes the abrasions around Tony's mouth and acidly poses the rhetorical question, "Hard to shave when you're stoned?" David informs that such marks may also be a result of someone placing an object over someone's mouth to smother him/her. David also points out signs of petechial hemorrhaging (burst blood vessels in the eyes), which can also happen under circumstances in which there is no foul play. Gil concludes from the visit to the morgue that" It's hard to OD on just inhaling heroin. I know he was restrained, which leads me to believe someone forced him to ingest lethal amounts of heroine and Xanax."

Back at the scene of the crime, uniformed officers are sealing off the front porch with police tape when a floozy blonde barges in like a moose, telling them that she has been answering stupid questions from reporters for hours, and that this is her house. Catherine asks Brass who she is and he says, "It's Braun's squeeze. She's an ex-stripper too. Perhaps you two met in a professional capacity?" Catherine ignores this slight and asks where she has been for the last twelve hours, and Brass says, "Quote, out, end quote." The blonde (named Janine) is then unceremoniously fingerprinted.

Catherine takes off from the crime scene and makes a beeline for a casino, where she manages to get an audience with Sam Braun just by dropping her own name. He comes down to the reception and together they stroll through the casino. He proceeds to reminisce about seeing her naked when she was a stripper and wanting to take her home with him even though he was married. Their walk down memory lane is interrupted by Sam's son complaining that reporters were disrupting the flow of valet parking. Sam dismissively sends him off and walks Catherine to a little bar, and muses fondly over the memory of his late son Tony. Catherine confronts him about Janine, who is a gold-digger. Sam agrees and laments that now that the body's cold, she'll be going after his assets and whatever she can get her hands on.

Back at the lab, Gil is sitting in front of a fume hood, preparing to lift fingerprints from the pill bottle. They match Janine's prints.

After commercial break, Warrick is excitedly getting prints off the heroin balloon and Grissom is complaining about the office coffee to Nick, and Nick is complaining about the bug bites on his leg to whoever will listen. As it turns out he sustained heavy bug bites while crawling through the foliage in Tony's yard. Gil instructs Nicky to coat the wound with nail polish, and on the way out, Gil and Nicky establish that Nicky lifted prints that place a human entering or exiting the residence via the doggy door.

In the morgue, David has collected the contents of Tony's stomach in a jar. The contents of his stomach indicate that he ate heroin and Xanax but there are no undigested pills in his system. David guesses someone smashed them up and dissolved them in red wine. Apparently there were fifty pills dissolved in the wine he ingested.

Out on the streets of Las Vegas, Warrick and Brass are having a little talk with Tony's old dealer. They learn that, contrary to Janine's previous reports, she did not leave

Tony's house the minute the dealer showed up, but stuck around long enough to give him thirty Xanax. This leads them to talk to Janine, who claims that she just happened to drop thirty Xanax down the sink.

Greg and Grissom, in the lab, are running a series of analyses. Greg explains that heroin has a half-life of nine-and-a-half minutes before metabolizing to the more chemically stable morphine. Tony Braun, however, didn't have enough of either Xanax or heroin in his system to kill him. Greg adds, however, that there is another way to take heroin, and that's through an anal suppository. Upon hearing this, Gil looks mildly disgusted.

Gil then meets up with Catherine, who has brought an actual mannequin into the office on Gil's orders, but has no idea why. He then tells her a long story of Burk and Hare, two 19th century figures who made a living by drugging people, suffocating them, and then selling the bodies to a teaching hospital. They apparently got away with it until a medical student at the teaching hospital saw his fiancée on the teaching table. Grissom and Catherine then opine about Tony's cause of death: Janine administered an overdose, but then the gardener showed up, and she panicked and realized she didn't have enough time for an overdose to take effect. Gil explains that Burke would lean on his victim's chest, covering his mouth and nostril, but when you're doing drugs, you're a slob, and when you're being manhandled, you're even sloppier, like this. They conclude that he was "Burked".

The next scene is of Blue Diamond, which is a desert. Brass comes over to a scruffy looking guy who is digging a hole, and asks this guy happens to be digging on private property. The guy says his name is Curt Ritten, and that he has an order from Tony to begin digging if Tony dies under mysterious circumstances. Brass orders him aside, and everyone files downstairs to check out the shelves and shelves of silver bullion that Curt has unearthed.

Back at CSI central, Sara's taking her duct tape out of the freezer and dusting for prints. Soon Warrick comes by with three rolls of duct tape found in Curt's truck. Sara asks Warrick why anyone would bury twenty-three tons of silver bullion in the middle of the desert. Warrick tells her that for the past twenty years, the value of silver's gone to nothing and the commodity brokers are going to charge a storage fee per troy ounce and there's only one thing worse than losing seven to eight percent on silver a year, and that's losing nine to ten percent because of a storage fee." Sara persists and asks

"What good's twenty-three tons of silver coupons when you're dead?" Warrick then looks down at the tape they've compared and gleefully says: "Oh, we got ourselves a positive association! Roll to tape, Curt to Tony."

Under questioning, Brass presses Curt into revealing that Curt built the underground vault, and he was on friendly terms with Tony, going over to the house to hang out and watch football.

This leads to the issue of a warrant, and Catherine a plainclothesman enter Curt's place. Catherine immediately walks over to a chair where a skirt is artlessly draped -- the same skirt Janine was wearing a few scenes ago, incidentally -- and says to the detective, "I thought you told me Carl's wife lives in Carson City?" "She does. They both do. He just stays here when he's working," he replies, staring at the skirt. Both of them freeze as they hear a door creak, and follow the sound to a bathroom door. Of course, it's Janine, who has been in the shower and didn't hear them enter.

Unfortunately, however, the prints on the tape don't match up either Curt or Janine. Not only that, but the prints for the doggie door came back for Walt Braun, Tony's brother and a pit boss at the Tangiers. All pit bosses, it turns out, are required to keep prints on file.

This means that they have nothing to hold Janine on, and they're going to hold Carl until he can post bail. They also need to deduce how duct tape from Curt's truck ended up around Tony's wrists without Curt's prints on it.

Gil hightails it to the Tangiers to ask Walt about his fingerprints on the doggie door. Walt tells him he was out with Tony and Tony forgot his keys, so he entered through the doggie door to let Tony into the house. Gil notes that Walt is furiously scratching at insect bites that look just like Nick's, and figures that Walt can be placed at the scene of the crime during the time of the murder.

In the next scene, Brass reveals that according to the terms of Sam Braun's will, his vast empire would go to Tony, who was supposed to share it with Walt. However, he cut Janine in on a large portion of the take. Sara concludes that Curt was digging up the silver to protect Janine's interest. The only clue not fit into the puzzle is the earring Sara found on the scene. Janine explains she employs a maid who vacuums every day -- except for her day off, which happened to be the day Tony was killed. Conclusion: whoever lost the earring did so while killing Tony. Catherine and Gil spin yarns on what woman would be present, have access to Curt's truck, and have motive⋯

It's the wife, Bonnie, working in league with Walt. Her prints are lifted off Curt's bail check and are found to match the prints on the duct tape. She and Walt worked together to restrain and sedate Tony, and then panicked when the gardener showed up, so they suffocated him. Bonnie lost her earring, and didn't notice until later.

Cut to Catherine walking with Sam, and he tells her sadly, "I loved one son more than the other⋯they're my sons. I made them, I raised them, and one kills the other." He then reminisces about the fact that Catherine's mom was his long time mistress and the episode is over.

Chaos Theory

Our episode opens in 1983, as a barely-covered woman wanders down the hall of a college dorm. A towel wrapped around her, she strolls past a group of fraternity pledges, the pledges practically trip on their own tongues, and the camera swoops over to a pizza delivery guy. The camera then focuses on a thin blonde staring out of the window into the rainy night, her reverie interrupted when her cell phone rings; she tells the caller she'll be right down. We get a shot of where "down" is and see a cab in a parking lot. We get a shot of the blonde at a window.

Cut to a sunny day. The camera pauses briefly on a plane ticket, then pans out to Brass and Gil walking down the hall of a dorm. "Paige Rycoff, freshman," Brass is saying. "Booked a one-way ticket to Boulder. Never got there. Four days MIA." Gil says, "Missing persons, the first twenty-four hours are gold. After that, quicksand." He and Brass walk into Room 410, and after excusing the photographers, investigators, and police officers, take a look around. Brass notes that Paige didn't take her suitcase, her purse, or the cab she called. We see another shot of the plane ticket to Boulder and learn that it's not refundable. Gil notes that there's no sign of struggle.

They continue their investigation after the credits roll with a review of the security measures in place for the dorm. There are apparently four security cameras per floor and a turnstile that prevents non-residents and non-students from entering. Sara comes in and announces that the scent dogs are coming.

Catherine and Nicky arrive, walking down the hall and wondering how they can possibly interview all four hundred residents within a reasonable period of time. Gil, however, instructs them to look through the footage from the security cameras.

Sara is in Room 410 with Gil, telling him that Paige made a note to have all her mail forwarded, including her security deposit. Gil tells us that Paige's roommate, Jennifer Riggs, left two weeks into the semester, and that someone spackled the walls with toothpaste instead of spackle. Gil notices a difference in color between certain parts of the floor and Sara muses that there might have been an area rug, which could have been used to haul a body out of the room.

After the dogs sniff around the halls, Warrick and
Catherine suit up to go down the trash chute. As Catherine
slides down, Nicky asks some security guard to see any
camera that covers Paige Rycoff's room. After the tape is
uncovered, Nicky and his security guard friend skip back
four days and Nicky immediately notices someone covering
the camera with a piece of fabric. Nicky slows the recording
down and does a frame-by-frame analysis. Nicky figures
out that somebody pushed off the wall and tossed
something on the lens.

In the trash chute, Catherine is slowly lowering herself
down and examining the walls while she chats with
Warrick. At one point she notices a red splotch on the wall,
and bids him to stop lowering her down. We see a red
substance on the rough walls. Catherine extends a finger,
swipes the wall, and smells the substance -- it's pizza sauce.
She continues down the chute until she hits the dumpster
and notes that the trash must get picked up every morning.
She then catches the scent dogs circling aimlessly and says,
"Hey, Warrick, looks like we're not the only ones chasing
our own tails."

Back in Room 410, Sara examines the room more carefully
and finds some stains on a mattress. She circles them with
a Sharpie. The camera switches to a shot of the four
security cameras. In one of the cameras, we see Nicky

looking up at the lens. We then watch Nicky printing the exact spot where the camera-coverer smacked his hand. Sara, meanwhile, has found DNA, blood and semen.

After Gil has to talk to Paige's hysterical parents, he retreats to his office to view the split-screen video surveillance. Catherine watches with him and they decide that it looks as though somebody was carrying out a rug. Nick, meanwhile, has procured a kid whose prints match those of the prints taken off the wall where the security camera had been covered. He admits he covered the camera and we get to see via flashback. The boys then get the frat boy to admit that he knew Paige; they had dated once or twice, and then Paige dumped him.

The Rycoffs, meanwhile, have gone to the press and are telling their story on prime time news. At the lab, Sara and Gil get the results of the tox screen from the blood, semen, and DNA Sara picked up off the mattress. They show rohypnol (a.k.a. "roofies"), and the DNA in question isn't Paige's. Sara tells Gil, "We may have two victims: one missing, one raped."

Catherine and Nicky are watching the tape of the parking lot to see what vehicular traffic is like. They have to recap the night, frame-by-frame.

The next day, Brass, Sara, and Gil visit Paige's ex-roommate Jennifer Riggs, who dropped out earlier in the year. She tells them what she remembers: there's a flashback scene of an unconscious Jennifer being carried into her bedroom by an unidentified male assailant. Jennifer notes that whoever did this to her lived in her dorm, and the assault was what prompted her to drop out.

Sara, Warrick, and Gil now need to collect DNA, which, if given willingly, can be used in court. They are, however, hoping someone refuses, thus giving him or her a suspect. A montage of swabbing college aged men follows. All of this swabbing leads to thirteen markers, thirteen matches, and one suspect.

Their first suspect, a baseball player, is exonerated because he was in Fresno for a game on the night that Jennifer was assaulted. Nicky and Catherine have noted a silver Volvo circling the parking lot over and over again. They find the one in question and find that it is registered to Robert Woodbury, a tenured philosophy professor. Gil then compounds the car and sends Catherine off to deal with the professor.

Catherine confronts him with the fact that he circled the parking lot six times. In the middle of the interrogation, a pretty, female undergrad stops in and gives Woodbury puppy dog eyes and he tells her he'll see her tomorrow. Gil notices a broken shard of pottery on the floor and picks it up with a pair of forceps, saying , "Some circumstantial evidence is as strong as when you find a trout in the milk" to which the professor replies "Henry David Thoreau." Gil loses it and says that if he has a legit reason for circling the dorm over and over would he please share it now? The professor, under the stink-eye of Catherine and her adultery radar, admits he and Paige were conducting an affair, but only in his office. He also admits that he went to the dorm the night Paige was to leave town, to say goodbye, but she didn't come outside.

At the lab, Greg is showing Nicky that the hair they found in the Volvo matches the hair from Paige's hairbrush, and the skin tags on the end indicate that her hair was ripped or pulled out. Woodbury, upset, denies that Paige was in his car. A phone call from his house to Paige's phone was made when he was in a staff meeting so the CSI team wonders if Mrs. Woodbury was the one who made the phone call and shared a car ride with Paige. Mrs. Woodbury confirms the story not long before Paige's body is found in a trash compactor.

Catherine is almost in hysterics—since the trash chute looked ok she didn't check the dumpster. The coroner, however, tells them she may have been dead before she was placed in the compactor: she was killed by massive internal bleeding; Paige's spleen ruptured from some sort of blunt force trauma, and her ribs were broken. The CSIs make a beeline to the dumpster. Warrick finds blood; Nicky finds a fresh dent on the dumpster with vehicle paint chips. Nick opines that the whole thing might have been a hit-and-run and Warrick wonders if someone tossed Paige's body in the dumpster after hitting it.

At the lab, they discover that the paint chips were from a custom paint job and are able to narrow down the possible cars in the area. Warrick points out that the blood he found matches Paige's, and Brass has the owner of the custom paint job car in the office. The suspect was hurrying home in response to his nine-months-pregnant wife's pager summons. He swerved into the dumpster to avoid a van. In the SUV and there's no hair, blood, or fibers, so they let him go.

At this point, Gil decides to re-enact what happened. She was in her dorm room, and she ended up in a dumpster. Everyone returns to the dorm. Sara plays Paige, and notes that the trashcan is missing. Gil borrows an RA's trashcan; Sara tries dumping it in the chute but almost dumps the trashcan with it. Gil enlists a random freshman to help them play out the scenario; the freshman is to count to a hundred and then drop the can down the chute. Gil and

Sara are waiting for it as it comes down. They theorize that Paige dropped the trashcan down the chute. She wanted her security deposit back, so she came back down to retrieve the can. She and leaned into the dumpster -- it got hit with her pinned behind it, and she got crushed, then fell into the dumpster, injured. Paige then bled to death in the dumpster.

Gil relates this to the Rycoffs and they are upset that it was no one's fault; just and accident. They threaten to hire a detective to find out what "really" happened, and storm out of the room.

Overload

We open with a construction scene. A pick-up truck stops, and its driver is chatting with the foreman when a hard hat, and then a person, crashes down onto the windshield of the pickup.

Gil soon arrives and the Sheriff, already on the scene, wants to know what he's doing here since it's a suicide— duh. Gil wants to know why someone suicidal would bother coming in to work.

Credits roll and we return to the show to see Gil riding in an industrial looking elevator, sporting a hard hat. The Sheriff is along for the ride, explaining that the construction site will, upon completion of the project, host a jail. . "Fourteen hundred beds means fourteen hundred criminals off the street. The old jail's maxed. The prison population's increased by ten percent in one year," Ike posits. Gil asks the foreman if he gets a bonus for early completion, and indeed he does to the tune of $20,000 per day, and he is currently ten days ahead. The elevator stops and we learn that the dead guy's name is Valenti, and Valenti had the entire floor to himself, as he was the safety guy who drilled holes for the safety cables.

Gil examines the floor where Valenti worked and calculated that he would have hit the ground in under five seconds if he jumped or fell off of that floor. He looks down at the blood at the spot where Valenti must have jumped off, and notices the drill that's still hanging from the edge of the platform. He examines it and says that the drill is shorted and shocked Mr. Valenti. He then asks a rhetorical question: did they think he jumped before or after he was shocked? The foreman insists that something called a ground fault circuit interrupter would have prevented such a thing. In this case, since the third prong of the power plug was cut off, the drill was no longer grounded, and the GFCI did not kick in.

Gil then wanders over to Mr. Valenti's toolbox, and shares with us that the wire cutters may have been used to tamper with a grounding prong; he then takes prints from the cutters.

Elsewhere, Catherine and Nicky greet O'Reilly the detective about a 419. The deceased is fourteen-year-old Dylan Buckley. He ended up, for some reason, on the floor of the office of Dr. Leigh Sapien. Apparently, he had reactive attachment disorder, and issues with his mother and she'd been treating him for six months. Dylan was apparently complaining about his curfew when he went into a seizure. He hit his head, and the seizure stopped, she said, when he was dead. Nick mmhmms and lifts some beige fuzz from her white suit.

At the morgue, Gil learns that the only three human bones not shattered or broken in Valenti's fall were the malleus, anvil and stirrup. Gil and David argue briefly when David tells him that there was no physical evidence of electrocution. David checks again to make sure, and concludes that nope, he wasn't electrocuted. Or at least, there is no physical evidence to suggest he was. Gil still disagrees.

Sara finds this puzzling—he always taught them that the evidence doesn't lie, and in this case, there's no evidence. He says "Just because we don't see something we're supposed to see doesn't mean it's not there." He goes back to examining the inner workings of the faulty drill, and notes that the wires in the drill have been crossed and the polarity reversed. The crossed wires confirm that someone tampered with the drill. Now, the question is why Valenti was fried. Sara still remains confused: the soles in Valenti's rubber boots should have protected him. Gil takes the boots from Sara and finds a nail in the sole of one of the boots.

Warrick, meanwhile, is matching the prints Gil lifted from the cutters. The prints have been ID'd: Mr. Harris, the foreman. Gil immediately goes to question Mr. Harris, but the Sheriff remains hyper present. He tells Gil: "This is how it's going to work: the construction site is going to re-open and the investigation is going to go away." Gil heartily agrees that this will be the case—AFTER his lab processes all the evidence. Brass knocks on the door and Gil exits. We learn that Valenti was a union rep who, three days prior to his death, demanded more overtime pay and pressed for a walkout. Gil listens intently to this, as well as to the knowledge that the Sheriff and Harris go way back and the Sheriff was Harris' best man. He returns and tells the Sheriff and Harris what he learned about Valenti's interest in getting paid more.

Meanwhile, Nicky is going through Dylan's clothing. He gets to the boy's white boxers, and notices more of the same beige-colored lint he found on Sapien's sweater. Nicky questions the boy's mother, and her story matches Sapien's. Nicky pays a visit to the coroner and we learn that Dylan has skull fractures that seem consistent with grand mal seizures. He also has bruises all over his torso, and none of those beige linty things are anywhere on his clothes. They conclude that there may have been a moment where the boy was in nothing but his boxers.

Gil is walking into the CSI offices when a man comes out of nowhere to offer him useful information. He says, "I was the union rep before Roger. The walkout was my idea. Bob Harris threatened me and my family. I wouldn't betray the union so I gave up my position at the local; Roger picked up where I left off." Gil wants to know why this man was telling him this. The man says: "that could have been me."

Greg appears not long after Gil's brief conversation with the union rep. Apparently, all those tan fibers were angora, which is goat hair that has been spun, washed, and dried.

Gil demands to see the body again and David accompanies him to check it out. Valenti's troponin levels were up; Gil notes that the enzyme's levels typically rise after ventricular fibrillation, which could be indicative of electrocution. Valenti also had six to seven times the normal level of iron in his blood, and he was jaundiced.

Next scene: Gil opens the door to the prep room of the mortuary, and asks the mortician, Gessig, if he's begun prepping the body yet, and asks to see his testicles. Gessig is not in favor of this, and says, "If I let you see them, I have to let everybody see them" but eventually relents. Gil reaches under the sheets, comments that his testes were as big as skittles, and tells us all about hemachromatosis -- the result of ingesting trace amounts of iron in his blood over a long period of time. Gil gets a pint of Valenti's blood. At CSI central, Sara shares her own news: the cutters didn't match the serrations on the plug, so someone else had to be responsible for tampering with the drill.

Nicky and Catherine, meanwhile, get the down low on Sapien she got her license suspended for having sex with a patient that was a minor.

In the meanwhile, Gil has tested Valenti's blood and has learned that there is enough iron in it to complete a circuit.

In questioning, Catherine and Nicky break out the big guns: Catherine comes out with the angora blanket in question, and Nicky has a flashback in which Sapien tumbles with her underage, now-dead patient on the blanket. She denies it and they remind her of her license suspension. She explains: "I was a resident, he was seventeen, we were in -- look, no criminal charges were filed. It should have been expunged from my record." They leave with the blanket and Nick looks upset.

Gil further develops his theory using a pickle and we learn that Valenti's body was turned into one big, non-resisting, highly conductive wire. To quote Sara: "In through his hand from the drill, out through the nail in the boot." Greg bursts in with print results from the nail that was found in the shoe.

At the lab, Nick is swabbing the entire blanket and is interrupted when Catherine comes in: she had the lab test Dylan's blood for elevated levels of creatine kinase, an enzyme linked to a post-seizure state, but his levels were normal. Nicky then tells Catherine why he is so emotionally involved in this case: as a nine-year-old, Nicky was molested by a babysitter. Later, the swabs he meticulously collected from the blanket have borne fruit: they have yielded three distinct sets of epithelials: Sapien's, Dylan's, and Dylan's mother's.

Back at the case of the electrocuted construction worker, we learn that Ian Wolf's prints are on nail in the boot.

While this is going on, Catherine and Nicky learn from David that angora is all over Dylan's nasal passages and lungs. They opine that Dylan's mother, in an effort to deal with his reactive attachment disorder, decided to try rebirthing therapy. This led to her wrapping him in a blanket and accidentally smothering him.

In the construction worker case, Wolf is arrested and everyone who survived this episode lives happily ever after.

Bully For You

This episode begins in the corridors of a high school. One boy uses a spray can to write "stick" on someone's locker before going to the little boys' room. The mirror to his right explodes and he ducks as five bullets fly into his back. He falls to the bathroom floor, dead.

Brass, as usual, is among the first on the scene and acts as narrator so we know what's going on: the deceased is named Barry Schickel. His wallet is still on him, and he is noteworthy because he was recently voted class clown. They decide that because the victim was shot in the back, the perp is a coward.

In the hallways, Catherine stops a janitor from scrubbing away the graffiti that the boy left shortly before dying in the bathroom. Elsewhere in the school Brass is conducting interrogations and learns that Schickel was a member of the football team and was just coming out of practice. In the bathroom, Gil is inspecting the point of impact on the mirror and digs out a bullet.

Meanwhile, a helicopter is skimming over the desert, piloted by Nicky and Sara. Suited up in goggles and other safety equipment, they rappel to the sand and rock below.

They are there to inspect and airlift a body that is in a big red gym bag.

Meanwhile, Catherine and Warrick catch up with Gil in the boys' room, and Catherine notices a smudged thumbprint on a bathroom stall door, orange, like that of the paint on the locker. Catherine immediately recalls that the spray-paint on the locker is orange, like the paint in the thumbprint. She takes off to look at the locker again while Warrick and Grissom map trajectories to figure out where the shooter was standing. We are treated to a fuzzy reenactment of the kid being shot in the back while he stood at the urinal, and they decide the shooter was 5'3 or 5'4.

Back at CSI Central, the big red bag with the body in it is getting X-rayed Sara sees a coin she pegs as a half-dollar but David corrects her—it's a silver dollar. Nicky pegs a medical implant, and David notes a plate in the guy's head. Sara pushes to open the bag and David says that he already can tell that the guy in it has been dead for two months.

As Catherine checks out the locker, a blonde passer-by tells her that it's "Dennis Fram's locker". The blond, as it turns out, is the school counselor, and takes an attitude that Catherine quickly shuts down by noting that one of her charges is dead, shot by another one of her charges.

Warrick, meanwhile, is playing with beeping walkie talkie looking thing that Gil identifies as a polymer-sensor proboscis. This fun toy is about ten grand, and they debate the merits of using it, versus using good old fashioned forensics. Naturally Gil is on the side of the traditional methods of crime solving and he tells Warrick that the proboscis' services will not be needed.

Gil goes to see what Catherine has found out about the locker. She learned from the guidance counselor that Dennis always picked on Barry but Barry (according to same counselor) would never, ever have retaliated. Dennis Fram is soon dragged into the counselor's office for questioning. Gil then opens up his forensic fun kit and tests the shirt for gunshot residue, which he finds on Dennis's shirt. Dennis tells Brass that he happened to be at a shooting range the night Barry Schickel was killed. His sister will be happy to confirm the veracity of his alibi. As if on cue, his older sister bursts in, refusing to be cowed by Brass or Gil.

Back to the red gym bag: as soon as David unzips it Sara gags and Nick looks as if he'd like to. David hauls out a blackened, bloated, dismembered arm. David also extracts the guy's head and a gambling chip. The last item David pulls from the bag- a jacket dripping with the remains of human flesh. The rest of the body is bones and goo. David points out that a stew of rotted flesh can smell up a place permanently, so it's best to burn the body. Sara and Nicky take the chip and the jacket and beat it out of the autopsy room as David disposes the rest of the remains.

Warrick, meanwhile, is on the floor of the boys' bathroom, using a mortar and pestle to improvise absorbing agent. Catherine comes along and asks what he's doing, forcing Warrick to explain: he's using the air pump to disturb the air in the sample area, causing the air gets drawn down into the glass tube, and the shock of the air's entry activates the absorption medium below, so the molecules suspended in air get trapped. Catherine seems unimpressed.

Later, Barry's body is in the morgue and Gil is listening to David's reports of bullets and trajectories. Ever observant, he notes that the placement of the bullets doesn't match the internal damage Schickel suffered. David notes that this kid is a special case: "All his internal organs are on the opposite side of typical placement."

Sara, meanwhile, has extracted enough decomposed flesh from the jacket to be able to read the nametag: W. Cartsen. She is, apparently, undeterred by the fact that the jacket could have been picked up at a thrift store or Salvation Army. Nicky fishes a mystery item out of the jacket and Sara hurls again.

Just then, an Emergency Services guy appears. Sara met him in the desert when she picked up the gym bag holding a rotten corpse, and thought he was cute. Despite having thrown up several times, she manages to continue flirting with him after popping an altoid. He asks her if she can have dinner right at that moment since he's on his break. Sara declines—she is at work and can't drop everything because some guy asks her to go out with him because he happens to be on break. Their flirtation is short-lived: he smells the rotting corpse on her (and possibly puke) and says he needs to go out for air.

Gil is talking with the guidance counselor, wanting to know who might have hated Barry Schickel. Gil learns he was a bully. We meet the kid who stabbed him with a fork. He is pretty happy that his tormentor died but has an alibi, so didn't kill him. The counselor begins to blame herself for the kid's death, and Gil asks her if she's hiding something. She claims she isn't. He seems unconvinced.

Warrick, Nick, and Catherine are talking about what they used to be like in high school when Sara appears and summons Nick back to gym bagman patrol. They leave, and Warrick admits that he was bullied in high school pretty bad, so he kind of can understand why someone would want that kid dead.

The thing that Nicky found earlier is, apparently, a matchbook covered in human fat. The tech has still managed to figure out that the matchbook comes from Romanini's, a place Nicky characterizes as "a nightclub for boomers off the strip." As Nicky and Sara head out to investigate it, O'Reilly drops by to tell them that W. Cartsen is actually Second Lieutenant WilGreg Cartsen. He is apparently a Viet Nam veteran who was wounded in action.

Warrick, meanwhile, has completed his analysis of what exact smells are going around the boys' room. He picks up a printout and says, "I got a boatload of chemical compounds here -- marijuana, bubble gum, cigars. It's like every guy's bathroom in America" he says. "What doesn't belong?" Gil asks, then walks off.

Over at Romanini's, O'Reilly, Sara, and Nick show the manager a sepia-toned enlistment photo of W. Carter, asking, "Is this man a patron of your establishment?" The manager says he doesn't know until Nick describes him as a down-on-his-luck, Viet Nam vet who wore an army jacket. The manager then recognizes him: at some point, Cartsen became one of those crazy homeless people who spend hours at bars or coffee houses, talking to themselves. He said that Cartsen was ruining his business, so he tossed the guy a gambling chip and told him to cash it and then never come back. This happened, apparently, about two months ago, and he never saw the man again.

Gil is running a computer simulation of what happened in the bathroom when Catherine enters his office to tell him that she can put Dennis at the crime scene. She lifted his print from the locker and, thanks to the spray paint, can place Dennis at the crime scene during the time of the shooting. Brass, who's accompanied her to Dennis' house, asks his parents if he can inspect the two dozen weapons in the Fram home. Dennis immediately doubles over, apparently in pain, and his sister comforts him. She explains, "Dennis has a bleeding ulcer from being bullied by Barry Schickel." We flash to scenes of the horrific pranks inflicted on Dennis on a daily basis. She explains she used to beat up anyone who touched him, but now that she's in high school, the boys have gotten too big for her to beat down. Catherine asks, "How tall are you?" "Five-four...with heels," she replies.

Meanwhile, Gil, who seems to know everything about everything, is going on about floral top notes and the compounds that go into perfumes. The computer chugging away in the background beeps, and identifies the smell that Warrick felt was out of place for a men's room: Chanteuse perfume. Gil tells Catherine to get a warrant for the sister's perfume. In the next scene, Brass is interrogating her: she claims she was out driving around during the Schickel murder and Brass asks, "So, what, your perfume just wafted in the boys' room off Highway 10?" Warrick tries to explain how the aroma "fingerprint" they isolated in the bathroom is that of Chanteuse, she wears Chanteuse, and this makes her their prime suspect. The sister, who is named Kelsey, says she wears that perfume cause her dead mother wore it, and gets snippy. Her father informs CSI that this is a weak argument and drags his daughter off.

Sara and Warrick return to talk to the manager once again. Under questioning, they got him to admit that he shoved Cartsen in a large duffel bag, zipped him up, and rolled the bag down a very steep hill, figuring he'd wake up when he sobered up. Alas, he did not.

At CSI central, Dennis appears, wanting to talk to Gil. He explains that he had gone back to the school to pick up a book; he registered the spray-paint on his locker, then went to the bathroom. While he was in a stall, he heard the mirror shatter and saw Barry get shot. Just then, Brass comes in and asks for a moment with Catherine and Gil: it turns out that Kelsey slept with Schickel's football coach as leverage for asking him to intervene. Who, then, did Dennis hear shoot Barry? As it turns out, it's the guidance counselor. She feared that Barry Schickel might have incited someone to kill so she would juts kill Schickel herself was a way to prevent someone else from going V-Tech on the place. Gil reveals that she was the assistant principal at Tetrick High school in Arizona: Eleven kids were shot after Columbine. "I watched them die at my feet, just because some sophomore couldn't take the jokes about his glasses," she says. Gil suggests she has post-traumatic stress disorder from this; she shakes her head no, saying, "I did this for my kids."

Meanwhile, Sara showers with lemons, Nicky is signing out Cartsen's belongings, saying, "Rest in peace, Lieutenant", and Gil filling out a grant form for funding to buy the Cyranose 320; he fumbles for stamps in his disorganized desk, and Catherine stops in only long enough to extract a roll for him and then leave silently. As Gil seals the envelope, Warrick stops in the doorway, goes to say something, then thinks better of it, drifting off and leaving Gil alone.

Scooba Doobie Doo

The episode opens with someone preparing to show an apartment to a couple. The mood is dampened when they open the door to the apartment and blood is all over the walls.

The next scene: Brass surveys the apartment and mutters, "I worked in a slaughterhouse one summer, looked a lot like this." Moving on, he apprises us of the situation. "The lease is in the name of one Clifford Renteria. He lived here with his girlfriend 'til they snuck out in the middle of the night." Gil points out that the blood on the wall could be not human, but a quick test with a little kit that apparently is for the purposes of sorting human blood from non-human blood confirms that it is, indeed human. Gil surveys the apartment and says that since the human body has eight quarts of blood, whoever did this is probably dead.

The credits roll. Gil, Sara, and Warrick are in the apartment, wearing blue jumpsuits, and spraying with luminol. Sara begins snapping pictures while Warrick continues to try to identify what may have been lying on the carpet, protecting a small swatch of it from being sprayed.

Meanwhile, there's a fire swirling over the dry brush in the mountains. Nicky and Catherine are walking toward a gaggle of firefighters and are immediately instructed to direct their attention to the fact that there is a scuba diver in a tree. Nicky haltingly tries to explain it away by saying that Lake Mead is over the hill and the helicopters are dropping water. Catherine feels it's ludicrous that a scuba diver could get scooped up by a helicopter but Nicky persists.

At the apartment, Brass and Gil are questioning the landlord and find out that the leaseholder's ex girlfriend disappeared three months before, and that in any case, he's not getting his deposit back.

Back at the fire site, Catherine lays down a yellow plastic marker at a cracked pressure gauge from an air tank, then photographs it. Nicky, meanwhile, is staring at a pristine, unburnt patch of green grass, wondering how it escaped incineration. While staring, he also happens to see a cigarette tucked into a burnt-out book of matches, which he picks up with a plastic spatula. He then coats the matchbook with aqua-net, ensuring that it won't crumble.

Brass and Grissom, meanwhile, are interviewing Cliff Renteria, platform head at Monaco receiving. He begins the interview by inquiring as to the whereabouts of Allison

Scott. Cliff says Allison has left Vegas. Grissom tells him that the apartment she vacating had been the victim of a gory act of vandalism. Cliff immediately spills the beans by giving them the scoop on the apartment manager: "He had it coming, I'll tell you that right now. Apartment stank, there were flies everywhere, no water. So I trashed the place." Not satisfied with this, Grissom asks for an explanation as to whose blood is on the walls and why. Cliff tells them he has nose bleeds constantly from Hep C. Gil still wants to make sure he's got the story straight: "You expirated blood through your nose all over your apartment walls to get back at your apartment manager?"

Cliff confirms that this is indeed the case and Gil and Brass speak privately for moment. Gil isn't convinced he's telling the truth—blood coming out of one's nose on a trajectory towards a wall would make an oval shaped pattern but the patterns on the apartment wall are v-shaped. They ask if they can examine some of the furniture that came from his old apartment after Gil notes both an electric saw and a lamp with a bloodstained base. Cliff shrugs that Gil can take whatever he wants, as it will save him rental fees—he's currently living in a truck.

Sara and Warrick then paw through his stuff, but there isn't any blood anywhere. They then test electric saws for blood smatter patterns while listening to music.

Later, Gil receives what appears to be a disappointing result from the lab, and calls Renteria in for questioning again. He patiently explains to Cliff that he can't really sign off on a case until he understands it, and asks how he got the idea to blow blood all over the walls and exactly how long it took to collect it all in the first place. Cliff admits it took about a month and even volunteers to show Gil and Brass how it worked. He tacks up a piece of newspaper to the blackboard, tells Gil and Brass to back up, and then lets the blood fly.

Sara and Warrick have concluded that blood spraying from a saw would indeed make V-shaped patterns. Gil admits that Cliff manages to expel blood in roughly the same pattern by standing very close to the wall and blowing almost sideways. Just as they are all about to write off the case as a nosebleed, the lab tech races in the room and says that the lamp they took from him has a woman's blood on it—not his. Sara theorizes that it could be his girlfriend's since she is missing.

Over at plot B: Catherine and Nick drop by the morgue and learn that the scuba diver stopped breathing before the fire started. Catherine speculates the man was probably killed someplace else and dumped. Nicky still thinks that he might have fallen out of a helicopter scoop but the coroner disabuses him of that notion: the victim's injuries are inconsistent with a fall of that nature. Still, when he learns that the victim died of a heart attack, he resuscitates the theory, arguing that perhaps he had a heart attack when he found out he was in a helicopter scoop about to be dumped over a raging wildfire. Again, Catherine poo-poos it. The coroner tells him that he died of cardiac concussion, and that he has a soapy residue on his skin. However, because a wetsuit has a snug fit and neoprene fabric, it's easier to get in and out of it if the skin is coated in dishwashing liquid. They then examine the air tank, and it's full, and at 3000 PSI. After a little research, Nicky learns that the tank exploded; Nicky is off and running to get the tank serial number, then use that to track down the renter of the tank.

Meanwhile, Sara and Gil charge back to the bloody house. They shine a flashlight all over the walls and scrape blood off the walls. There's no evidence of layered blood splatters. Sara continues to insist that Cliff blew blood all over the walls to cover up the death of his girlfriend, but Gil isn't buying it. They continue exploring the apartment, deciding to follow a flock of flies to a vent in the kitchen from which they flew in the house.

Catherine and O'Reilly pay a visit to an apartment inhabited by a young man named Jerry Walden who first attempts to tell them to beat it because he thinks they are solicitors. He changes his tune when Catherine introduces herself as a member of the Las Vegas crime lab, but doesn't let them in until Catherine asks him if he's missing a scuba tank. Apparently he is—he's missing it because it was found in the possession of one Bruce Skeller who in turn was found in a tree. Catherine asks why an experienced diver needs to borrow a tank; Jerry rebuts that experience and equipment do not go hand-in-hand. Being experienced and being a freeloader are not mutually exclusive. Catherine notes that a coffee table seems to be missing, and Jerry says it's being refinished. Crouching down to examine the splinter marks on the floor, Catherine suggests that perhaps it needed more than refinishing.

Gil and Sara are doing what Gil does best: studying the eggs of the flies that are inhabiting the Hep C apartment. Gil finds something—a silphib beetle—that usually feeds on rotting human flesh. Gil asks the apartment manager, Mr. Evans, who has been hovering nearby, and asks if he could get permission to break into the apartment walls since the original warrant didn't cover that. Evans wants to know if they'll pick up the replastering costs; Sara tells him he can submit a reimbursement form to the city. Evans, probably well versed in the celerity with which cities and other governmental agencies handle paperwork, declines. Gil and Sara decide to see if they can extract any DNA from the beetle. In a couple scenes, they take it to the lab and learn that it gave them enough information that they have been issued a warrant to knock down the walls. And off they go.

Meanwhile, Catherine is having a rendezvous with the building inspector from last season. She is pestering him to get her a land permit to check out property owned jointly by two men, Jerry Walden and Bruce Skeller. At the time that they bought the land, it was fifty grand an acre. Two years later, it skyrocketed in price and the two men refused to sell until last week. As it turns out, Jerry was all for selling, but Bruce was not, as he was a tree hugger. At the lab , Catherine takes the deed to the tech to be examined. Using a VSE-4 machine, he can make different signatures disappear at different light wavelengths, as different inks correspond to different wavelengths. They peer at what his machine uncovers.

Sara, and Gil finish knocking down a wall, Brass strolls in with a willowy blond and introduces her as Cliff's girlfriend, Allison Scott. Allison reveals that she left Cliff and in the process, she stubbed her toe on the lamp, thus explaining how that particular splotch got there. After Warrick leaves to draw blood from Allison, Gil and Sara share hangdog looks. As Sara is asking a rhetorical question involving playing connect-the-dots, Gil bolts to ask Evans about the wall his apartment shares with the Hep House.

At the lab, the scuba diver plot is tied up neatly in the space of about twenty minutes when Greg procures and Nicky finds ash wood splinters in the corpse's back. The way the crime went down, as theorized by Nicky and Catherine: Bruce and Jerry were fighting, Jerry landed a punch that made Bruce's heart skip a beat and Bruce went flying into the coffee table.

As Gil and Sara walk into Evans's apartment, he hastily explains away the scented candles by letting them know there was rotting food in the garbage, and the replastered wall by informing them of rain damage. Gil, who does not have a warrant to search the entire apartment, just the wall, is about to ask permission to look around when Brass arrives and informs them that Evans' wife has been missing, and they can break out the big guns with a big warrant. The camera then zooms in on a tangle of bugs in the vent that Evans shares with the Hep House and Sara finds a blanket with blood on it. The combination of these events has rendered Evan's protests mute.

At the CSI headquarters, Jerry's lawyer informs Catherine and Nicky they've got no evidence. Nicky rattles off the evidence to the contrary and tells them how he thinks it went down: "You had a dead body. So you decided to get creative. Fire season, wetsuit, liquid soap..." "You drove out to the lake, dumped the body," Catherine continues, "and lit up. Not 'cause you wanted a cigarette. You lit up with a purpose." Nicky tags in: "This gave you a head start. My guess is around the five-minute mark." "You figured the fire department would label it a hot spot," Catherine says, "relate it to the original fire, and the body would just burn up." . "A scuba tank contains compressed air. Too much heat and...kaboom," Nicky explains, and we get a re-enactment that features him flying through the air.

At Evan's house, knocking down the walls has borne little fruit. Gil and Sara share a bizarre and intimate moment outside when she rubs plaster from his face, and they then return inside. Gil tries to wash up but there is no hot water. Gil, who seems to know everything about everything, heads to the basement to check out the plumbing. Apparently the late Mrs. Evans is bobbing up and down in one of the water heaters, having been dispatched to the great beyond for "nagging" her husband.

The episode closes with Nicky and Sara asking Gil to breakfast. He declines and chooses to hang out with a beetle.

Alter Boys

It is Vegas at night and a Land Rover is gliding merrily along. A car is parked in an odd place and the driver of the Land Rover stops to walk toward the edge of the road. He hears a noise, and proceeds to hide by making his way down an embankment. His execution is not as graceful as he'd intended, and he slides down the embankment and lands on his stomach, next to a dead person. A young man in the process of digging a grave panics and runs, but is wrestled into the submission.

Seconds later, swarms of black and whites arrive in the desert. Gil and Nicky learn from Brass that the man digging the grave was named Ben Jennings. Ben Jennings, it should be noted, doesn't look particularly intimidating, and Nicky and Gil walk over. Nicky gets the ball rolling by asking him if he wants to explain what's going on. Apparently he does not. Gil seems unperturbed by this development, pointing to the corpse with his flashlight, and informing the silent Ben that the corpse will be happy to tell them anything they need to know.

Sara arrives as Ben is released from his handcuffs. She uses duct tape to lift samples from the soles of Ben's shoes. Gil and Nicky lift fibers off Ben's clothing, then examine his

body for defensive wounds. Ben stands still mute,
apparently terrified.

Meanwhile, on the strip: A black SUV pulls up at one of the
fancier casinos and Catherine and Warrick emerge, ready
to check out a dead body in found in the spa. Brass is there.
As usual, he provides the function of exposition, informing
the CSIs, and the audience at home, that "The body is
Shelly Danvers, D.O.B. 10/10/81. An employee walked in
to get towels, and found her here." " Warrick stares at the
body for a moment, splayed out on a locker room bench, a
magazine open beside her. Warrick departs to question the
night manager. She says she found the body when she was
restocking the locker room with clean towels. Catherine
asks her if she knows anything about re-dressing the body.
"Well, she was naked. I-I-I thought she should be covered,"
the manager says with hesitation, and continues, "Guests
were looking in. I put a robe on her. It's not like it's a crime
or anything." Warrick patiently explains that this casts a
shadow on his ability to figure out the circumstances
surrounding the death of the victim.

Back to our boy Ben Jennings: Sara is swabbing a white
powdery substance from the forehead of the body. Gil asks
if there are any fibers caught in the neck wound, and
indeed she observe some fibers in the wound--yellow
fibers, possibly satin. Gil points out that the corpse has a

dress shirt, but no tie. "Strangled with his own tie?" Sara muses. Gil merely replies, "Find me on the flour," having determined that the white substance on the victim's head is some variety of flour, and walks off.

In the more pleasant surroundings of a fancy hotel, Warrick and Catherine are perusing the spa reservations log and asking the spa manager if Shelley Danvers used the Jacuzzi at any time. She says no, Catherine points out that it's entirely possible for Shelley to have drowned in a Jacuzzi, and the manager, having lost her patience with the song and dance of criminal justice, snaps, "She did not drown on these premises." Warrick points out that they'll know whether or not Shelley did drown if they find water in her lungs and the manager rolls her eyes.

Back at CSI Central, the body has been identified as Oliver Dunne, a corporate lawyer and father of two. Apparently the widow Dunne had already paid a visit to ID the body. Gil points out that that he happens to be holding a .380 slug in his hand, and we get a visual of the way it had been lodged in his liver prior to its extraction. Gil asks David to confirm that the .380s embedded in Dunne's body aren't what killed him. David does so, noting that Dunne died of asphyxiation. Without oxygen to the lungs, the capillaries wither and dry up, and the pulmonary shuts down, thus confirming that he died of asphyxiation and not being shot.

Gil asks a rhetorical question as to why one would strangle old' Oliver with a tie and THEN shoot him several times. Sara enters and tells them all that the flour on the victim's head is a very, very fine flour used only in pizza ovens. Additionally, trace picked up some oregano in the sample, allowing her to nail down the flour to a certain pizza parlor. Gil looks stunned.

In questioning, Ben tells Gil he had a .380 but he lost it. Gil wants none of what he's selling and asks if Ben is employed. And indeed he is-- at Dante's Pizzeria, behind the Stratosphere, as delivery boy. Gil informs him that they found flour on the victim, and it's the kind used to make pizza. Almost gently, Gil says "Why don't you earn some points by telling me what the science is going to tell me anyway?" "Well, I don't have to talk," Ben reminds him, continuing: "If you know so much about these murders, what do you need me for?" Gil, who noticed that his youthful alleged perp said murders instead of murder, says slowly, "Murders? There are more bodies?" Ben looks sullen and reverts back to his former strategy of not talking.

At the scene of the crime, Nicky and Sara use radar and a laptop to find more bodies. They have dragged Ben with him and Gil continues asking him for information. Ben is still declining to give it. Sara eventually reads something interesting that seems to be a human silhouette. Gil attempts to unsettle Ben by giving him an up-close-and-personal play-by-play regarding how he feels when he's left the presence of a dead body, which prompts Ben to abandon his strategy of silence to say: "Mr. Grissom, I'm not a bad person." "You're not a bad person," Gil repeats, astounded. Ben shakes his head, looking like he's going to cry. "Then what are you?" Gil asks. Ben stands there, silent, as Gil walks away.

Meanwhile, at CSI central, Catherine learns that the victim didn't drown. David begins to muse about the possibility of heatstroke, and Catherine runs off to get a warrant that will allow her to search the spa. Before she accomplish this feat, she runs into Warrick, who has learned that Shelley was staying with a Tina Kolas. The two girls came to Vegas as part of a travel package. Catherine seems pleased by this turn of events.

Back in the desert, as law-and-order-types prepare to dig out another body, a man in a backwards collar approaches Gil to tell him that Benjamin is in his parish. He asks to talk to Ben. Gil seems disgusted but allows it, practically spitting out "When the reality of their actions set in, they usually turn to religion." The priest, faith unshaken, responds that there is no better time. Nicky and Sara, at this point, have pried the body from its grave. Nicky begins sweeping the dust off the body—who, judging by the contents of his wallet, is Kenny Ramiriez-- and Sara photographs it. The wounds are different from the ones on Dunne's body: Kenny had a big blow to the head that may or may not have been caused by a shovel. As they muse about motive and connections, O'Reilly arrives to tell them that they've found Dunne's and Ramirez's abandoned cars at an AmCon station off Highway 215. And off they all go.

Meanwhile, in a hotel room Catherine and Warrick are questioning Tina about the spa reservations Shelley had made. "We'd been drinking apple martinis for, like, three days straight." She continues, "Shelley said the spa would detox her, you know, clean her out". Warrick's eagle eye lingers over a shirt torn in half, and Tina to explain how this happened. She explains that they fought over it. A tug-of-war ensued and it ripped in two. Catherine takes the shirt as evidence, and asks how it is Tina can be sure that Shelley used only the dry sauna. Tina points her to the pad of paper by the phone and says that Shelley used it to make her reservation. Warrick says they're going to take the pad. Tina is confused, but surrenders it willingly.

At the gas station where Dunne and Ramirez's cars were found, Sara and Nicky are questioning the station attendant. He claims that he took a break without telling his boss to go out with a friend. When his buddy dropped him off, he noticed two cars, one of which had a blood puddle next to it. He took it upon himself to hose it away. Nicky and Sara are appalled.

Later, Ben's car is neatly covered with a plastic tent so Gil can examine it unfettered by the reality of the outside world. The priest appears, undaunted by Gil's hostility. We find out that Gil is a recovering Catholic. The priest tells Gil that Ben is a good kid who comes to church every Sunday. Gil, getting snarky, sprays luminol on the car, showing that it's soaked in blood. The priest doesn't believe Ben did this but Gil doesn't budge—the car has spoken and Gil has listened. The priest quotes something from the Bible at him and leaves.

Back at the other plotline, the spa manager is still giving lip to Warrick and Catherine, saying she has no record of who used the dry spa. Catherine dangles the notepad in front of her face and tells her that ESDA can look at this blank paper and see what's written on it, up fourteen layers. Warrick chimes in and tells her that a flashlight can often reveal pen impressions -- as in this case, where they've found a note on the pad that proves that Shelley logged an 8 p.m. appointment in the dry sauna. The spa manager feels that this is irrelevant but Catherine presses onward in the face of unwavering snottiness, informing the spa manager that Shelley died of a heat stroke. The sauna is kept at an optimal condition for a heat stroke -- 182 degrees—which could kill a person if left in there for longer than two straight hours. Brass, who has arrived, contributes to the discussion: "A hotel employee is supposed to check on the saunas every fifteen minutes. Regulations, right? We got a copy of the check-up sheet." The spa manager looks at Brass behind her, and Catherine and Warrick in front of her, and a look of panic flashes across her face.

She leads them to the pristine chambers of the tiled sauna, and Catherine asks what time the manager called 911. The manager launches into flashback: she came in to the sauna at closing time, ten p.m., which is when she discovered Shelley's body, moved her, put a robe on her, and called 911. To "protect the hotel". Catherine is astounded that she would try to protect the hotel from being charged with negligent homicide. "They drill into us that the reputation of this hotel is everything," the manager says. Catherine is unmoved.

So the crime scene at the AmCo is useless, but the bullets extracted from Ramirez and Dunne have matching striations that in turn match the .380 registered to Ben. The fibers from the wounds are 12-ounce merlot-poly, found in car upholstery matching the carpet in Ben's car. Gil reminds them that they have proved that Ben buried the bodies. But they haven't proved that he killed them: he wants the murder weapon, or evidence that Ben did more than bury bodies. Nicky says, " Let a jury decide. Anything else and we're playing judge. The evidence doesn't get any better than this." Gil acquiesces and tells them to ship the evidence to the DA.

At the casino, Brass tells Catherine that Tina is down playing quarter slots. She asks Brass why he thinks this case is not yet closed, and he says that a guy in the lounge told me Tina and Shelley were having a catfight over some guy named Jeremy the day that she died. He opines that's how the shirt really got ripped. Catherine agrees to re-examine the case before declaring it formally closed.

Gil and Nicky, meanwhile, discover Ben has a brother Roger with a long record: Armed robbery. Past convictions: breaking and entering, assault with great bodily harm. Paroled 9/27/2000. Gil dashes out the door and heads to Ben's cell in the holding area. "Tell me about your brother. We know that you only buried the bodies, so what happened -- did he threaten you?" he demands. Ben's breath comes out ragged but he says nothing.

We go next to Dante's Pizzeria, where we meet Roger as he furiously kneads a ball of pizza dough. "Did you learn to toss pizza in prison, Roger?" Gil asks. Roger mumbles something about how his brother got him the pizza job and he's staying clean. O'Reilly asks what Roger would think if he was told that Ben said he committed two murders. Roger says with confidence "He wouldn't do that." Gil then theorizes that right after work, Roger shot and strangled the victims. Roger is unwavering in his conviction and says: "Ben did it." He takes us through a flashback where Ben loses it and comes to him for help only to be turned down. Gil notes that whoever killed Dunne left flour on his face and we flash to Roger strangling Dunne. Gil informs Roger that when a person changes his mode of murder -- from gunshot to strangulation, for example, it's either for entertainment, or necessity. Roger repeats his assertion that Ben did it.

CSI then obtains a warrant to go through the trailer that the brothers share. Sara spots a dry-cleaning bag with the clothes intact and pulls out the contents of the bag: there's a stain on a denim shirt. Blood stains clothing even when the clothing is dry-cleaned. But so does pizza sauce. The impasse stands. Nicky continues to search the trailer's perimeter while Sara scrutinizes the stains. He immediately notices a steel drum full of coals and begins digging. Sara, meanwhile, uncovers hemoglobin, and Nicky finds a gun.

Cut to holding cells where the brothers Jennings are reunited. The lab results say that the dry cleaning baked in the stain, but it also degraded the blood to the point where there are no distinct or identifiable markers, and although the gun is the same, the barrel seems to have been altered, so the bullet striations are now different. Gil says they're going to present the evidence to the DA anyway; Nicky replies that Roger's going to walk free. And so he does. Roger strides out while his brother forlornly watches him go. Gil follows him and says, "The bullet jammed in the feed, didn't it?" We see Dunne's murder in flashback again. Roger smirks, the corners of his mouth turning up slightly, and walks off.

Back at the hotel: Catherine tells Tina that Shelley's autopsy results point to a severe allergic food reaction –in this case, to shellfish. Shelley, as it turns out, ate a seafood bisque, ordered for her by Tina after Jeremy called the girls' room and asked for Shelley. Shelley didn't know there was lobster in it, and ate it all. Tina insists that she didn't mean to kill her—she just thought that she would have an allergic reaction and not be able to make her date that night. Catherine explains how a food allergy reaction in a room heated to 182 is probably fatal. Warrick adds that as the allergic reaction worsened, her circulation failed. Tina sobs. Brass rolls his eyes and arrests Tina.

Gil learns that the DA's filing homicide charges against Benjamin and confronts the DA, who refuses to drop the case. Now there is more evidence against Ben: Roger just happens to have turned in the tie used in the murders, claiming that his brother forced him to hide it. Gil counters that Ben was set up. The DA says still refuses to drop the case.

Gil returns to jail to talk to Ben, telling him his brother turned in the tie. Dismayed, Ben coughs up the truth: "I just picked up the bodies at his place," he says, and he got Ben to pick up the tie so his DNA would be on it. He then told Ben: "You get into trouble, you don't have to say anything; I'm counting on you," and assured him that if he kept quiet, it would just blow over and go away. O'Reilly breaks the news to him that it most certainly is not going to go away, and that even under the best of circumstances, all Ben can look forward to is life without parole. Gil implores Ben to think of any physical evidence that might link Roger to the murders; there is none.

There is a montage to indicate the passing of time, and we learn that Ben gets the death penalty. Gil visits the priest and tells him he realizes he arrested the wrong brother. Then back to CSI, immediately seeing several deputies sprinting toward the holding pen where Ben is; the deputies are shouting frantically. He reaches Ben's and sees the young man convulsing, his arm covered in blood. He literally chewed his own wrist open and has succeeded in killing himself. The last scene is of Gil trying to stave off the bleeding, watching a wrongfully convicted man die in his arms.

Caged

A silver SUV driven by an angry looking woman barrels down a Las Vegas street, towards train tracks. The gates lower, a whistle warns that a train is coming, and she slams on the brakes. As the train slices down the track closer to her, the car hiccoughs forward for seemingly no reason, and she screams.

The car has been reduced to an accordion. Brass, as usual, is giving us the low down: "Megan Treadwell. I ran her plates -- thirty-three tomorrow." Catherine heads over to the train's engine and the SUV's door handle embedded in the metal—the point of impact is dead center. Gil asks, "The question is, 'Why did the SUV cross the tracks?'" Catherine replies: "To get to the other side."

The credits slide down the screen and when we come back, Catherine is climbing down the engine when Gil informs her that they are holding up trains all over the country by keeping the track closed and obstructed. As per the sheriff, Catherine has a little less than two hours to process the crime scene before the rails open up again. Gil walks off to head to another crime scene, giving Catherine the surely unwelcome news that Sara will be her partner for the case.

Cut to a shot of a picture book: the left side is an illustration and the right, a page of dense text headed by the word "cavil." O'Reilly fills Gil on what happened here: "Burglary in progress call. Once we made the entry, we found the victim downstairs," "Downstairs" is the lower floor of The Western States Historical Society. When they finish traversing the staircase, they are in a wood-paneled room lined with glass-fronted display cases and bookshelves. Gil says that he needs to know where the alarm was—apparently it was coming from downstairs where the body happens to be. They head down to a climate-controlled cellar filled with rare books. Gil and O'Reilly examine the body. Gil moves to adjust a book that's blocking his path, and he is instructed not to touch anything as the books are rare. The person giving the instructions, is, apparently, Aaron Pratt, the librarian and the only other person here when the alarm sounded.

They sit him down to ask him what happened. He says: " I always say goodnight to Veronica because I have to leave at 8:03 to catch the 8:10 bus. It's three blocks away. And sometimes, the bus comes at 8:08 so I have to rush to catch it." He rocks back and forth intently and sort of stares off into the distance as he recounts the challenges he faces with the Vegas public transportation. Aaron elaborates on his last conversation with Veronica, saying that sometimes she walks him to the bus. Gil asks if

Veronica walked Aaron to the bus that night and Aaron tells us she had to stay behind and finish working. Then a Uniball pen rolled across the desk, fell on to the chair, hit the floor and stopped rolling at the wastebasket. Water then fell into her eyes (by this he means sweat), and then that she grabbed her stomach, and seized like "Shelley's Frankenstein, up and down, flopping around like a salmon on my uncle's fishing boat." He continues that he couldn't help her because the cage was locked and he didn't have the key. Just then, Nicky enters. He has been assigned to this case and Warrick is dealing with a burglary.

Gil and Nicky excuse themselves and Nicky opines that Aaron is acting guilty, as opposed to acting autistic, which Gil thinks he is. Nicky can only relate to this via Rain Man and Gil explains that Rain Man was a savant whereas Aaron is a high-functioning autistic man with superior right-brain abilities.

Meanwhile, at the train wreck, a little dog joyfully trots towards Sara and Catherine, pausing to whimper at them and stare upward in that sweet, endearing way that only dogs can. The pooch is Maverick the dog, who lives on Martingale Street in Henderson, Nevada. Sara picks him up, coos and him, and tells him she'll take him home.

While Sara and Catherine pet the puppy, Brass talks to Clem the conductor. He says that the SUV just lurched forwards onto the track, and reminds Brass that the train has the right-of-way on the tracks. Sara interrupts as she comes by to ask the captain if the dog is his. It is not. And, as a coincidence, it shares the same address as the late Megan Treadwell.

At the morgue, we learn that Veronica did die of cyanosis, which means that blood was unable to oxygenate her tissues, which explains why she was blue in the face. The cause? David is still waiting on the blood tests but notes that he vomit in her throat, blood in her stool, hemolysis, irritation of the mucous membrane on her tongue. Gil thinks it's murder, as usual. David thinks it's a blood borne disease.

Nicky, meanwhile, is in the cellar dusting for prints when the curator, Stanley Hunter, introduces himself and scolds Nicky for causing damage to his precious books with dust and flashbulbs. As he wends on about the treasures in his cellar, Gil comes back from the morgue in time to inform Stanley that a rare book can also be evidence in a criminal investigation. Stanley is defeated. Gil, examining the floor, finds the Uniball pen Aaron spoke of, lying next to a trash can. Gil picks it up and says, "The good news, Nick? We had a camera in here?" Nicky reminds him: "There's no surveillance system." Gil replies, "There is -- Aaron Pratt. We just have to figure out how to get the film out of his head."

After a commercial break, Catherine and Sara continue planting numbered cones and taking pictures of the wreckage. Catherine notices a piece of headlight, appraises Sara of its presence, and pockets it. Meanwhile, Sara's noticed that one set of skid marks is going forward, but there's a second, darker set. It appears as though tires were spinning in place, in reverse.

In the cellar, Gil is asking about the chemical composition of the book-restoring fluids. Stanley tells him that the somewhat-acidic pages of old books are neutralizes by a solution with basic Ph. Primarily they rely on Imidazole, which is fifteen percent ammonia. He also fills Gil in on the fact that all rare books were kept in a vault. If they were to be read, the book was then taken to a room upstairs; otherwise, the book was restored in the cellar. We also learn that the book Veronica was restoring as she died was a British botany text from 1787 worth an estimated $300,000.

After Gil finishes with Stanley, O'Reilly pulls Gil aside to say that not only was Aaron first on the scene, he was also pinching several rare books. Gil nods thoughtfully and approaches Aaron and says, "'But I will wear my heart upon my sleeve for daws to peck at. I am not, what I am.'" "Othello, scene I, lines 61 and 62, Iago to Rodrigo," Aaron responds. Gil then asks how Othello found its way into Aaron's briefcase and Aaron eventually tells Grissom that Mr. Hunter doesn't like him, and Mr. Hunter breaks rules all the time. These rules range from eating lunch in the office to having an affair with Veronica in his office.

At the scrap yard, Sara and Catherine are examining the silver SUV and Sara's noting that the filament Catherine found is from a different car. At the back of the vehicle, Catherine's made note of both a paint scrape on the bumper and worn away rubber on the right rear tire. Meanwhile, Sara finds a cell phone in the driver's side wheel well, and a bag of dog treats. She also notices that the car's emergency brake is on and wonders if there was a second car that rear-ended her, and the conductor of the train failed to mention it because he simply didn't see it. They take to examining parts of the car under magnifying glasses and learn that that there's no glass on the filament Catherine found at the accident site, which indicates the lights weren't on.

Elsewhere in Vegas, Nicky and Gil are going through his apartment. Aaron goes berserk because Nicky dared to touch his mail, and Gil sends him to get a glass of water so he can speak privately with Nicky. He invites Nick to notice that everything's in precise order and his whole life is based on routine, without which he can't function. Aaron returns from the kitchen when Nicky excuses himself to search the bedroom. He asks Aaron how rare books got into this apartment. Aaron said that Veronica brought them and offered information about his personal life: "We date. We have dinner -- roast beef, baked potato, organic broccoli, Acacia pinot noir. Shakespeare in Love, DVD, Miramax. MCMXCVIII." He then enumerates that which makes him appealing to women, particularly Veronica: "I have a master's degree in library science and an English degree from UNLV. Some people like Mr. Hunter treat me like a freak. But Veronica didn't. She loved me. Not him." Gil is interrupted when Nicky beckons him to Aaron's room to see the creepy shrine Aaron has made for Veronica. Gil then quotes Shakespeare: "'Yet she must die, else she betray more men. Put out the light, and then put out the light.'"

Elsewhere, Catherine and Sara are parsing the 911 call Megan made shortly before her death. It beings with "Oh my God, you've got to help me. Please, help me. I'm in my car, there's this maniac and he's following me!" and concludes with a train whistle in the background and a dog's yipping. They replay the call over and over and magnify the background until they can hear the sound of her car being rear ended. We hear the car careen forward while the brake is activated -- and Catherine looks upset and leaves.

Nicky gets the results of Veronica's blood test and they are not good. Greg has identified ricin, a plant-based biotoxin. Nicky freaks out as he spent a long time in the same cellar where Veronica died. Greg rattles off a list of symptoms he'd be experiencing: sweats, cramps, convulsions—Nicky has none and is in the clear and should start looking for powders if he wants a sample of the ricin on the scene.

Over on Plot 2: Catherine and Sara have managed to reconstruct the details of Megan's last day alive. That morning, she and Maverick went to work, then she picked up some gourmet doggie treats. While in the parking lot, Megan accidentally backed into the car of an accountant named Croft, as identified by a barista at the coffee shop near the dog treat store. He instructed her to pull her head out of her ass; she threw her coffee cup out the window, and then he proceeded to follow her.

At the lab, Gil is looking at the book Veronica happened to be working on. It happens to be opened to an image of the plant from which ricin is derived. He sends for Aaron to come in and get questioned in the interrogation room. He, as it turns out, has heard of ricin. Gil informs him that he found Aaron's fingerprint on one of the pages of the book. He says immediately, "Page 153. I don't touch that book anymore." Why? Well, Aaron is happy to elaborate: it doesn't feel right. Gil asks Aaron if he told anyone about the difference in page texture. Indeed he did and Veronica replied that books feel that way after they've been restored, and Stanley kicked him out of his office. Then Stanley and Veronica fought; he hit her but they quickly seemed to make up. He offered her a salted hard-boiled egg; she declined. Gil, who has realized that Veronica was forging the books, asks Aaron to take him through the last moments of Veronica's life again. He does:

Catherine and Sara immediately locate Croft, who claims to have sold his black Excursion, which Sara and Catherine immediately procure. Catherine finds coffee all over the driver's side and the dash, and a coffee cup with lipstick on the lid, confirming that she threw her coffee at him. He chased her till she had to stop for the train, and then ran her into the train's path.

In the last scene, where we wrap up plot A: Gil tells Aaron that Veronica made the forgeries, left the originals at Aaron's house so he could take the blame if necessary, then intended to kill Stanley with ricin, but accidentally killed herself. Ricin, chewed up pens, and castor beans found at Aaron's apartment lead us to believe that he was to be the fall guy. The episode ends with Aaron tearfully telling Gil that he loved Veronica, and didn't kill her, and Grissom agrees.

Slaves of Las Vegas

Two youngsters frolic in a Las Vegas playground, merrily enjoying themselves, until one finds herself staring at the face of a corpse half buried in the sand.

Gil and Brass arrive and quickly determine that the body was killed somewhere else, and dumped there. Brass marvels at Vegas' tendency to induce idiocy: with miles of desert for the taking, why hide a body in a sandbox? According to Gil, the perp put it there so it would be found.

Upon Catherine's arrival, she and Grissom ponder how to extract the body from the sand without destroying any evidence left in the sand. Gil and Catherine carefully dig the body out, making sure to sift through the sand as they do so. Eventually, unearthed her and Catherine and Gil pace in circles.

And of course, there is a B plot. A car pulls up in front of a check-cashing storefront and Sara and Warrick are greeted by a detective, who in Brass' absence, is providing the details: "Gunshot victim, shipped to Desert Palms. Sante Cherna, thirty-two," Sante was shot in the leg as he was leaving to take the store's deposit to the bank, as he did the same time each week. Sante's sister was a witness and before interviewing her, Warrick and Sara split up to check out the store and its perimeter. saw the whole thing go down, and then Sara and Warrick split up -- she's going to do a once-around on the premises, and Warrick's going to begin checking out the parking lot.

After being dug out of the sand, murder victim A is being photographed on the autopsy table. She has bruises all over her back, and a tiny piece of a sticky black substance is lodged in a wound. After the body is rinsed, the coroner notices lacerations around the wrists. He then proceeds to make moulds of the wounds.

Meanwhile, Warrick notices a flyer on the ground although the same flyer has been safely and neatly pinned behind the windshield wipers of the other vehicles in the parking lot. They deduce that whoever hit Sante was an amateur— he or she grabbed the money bag and ran, leaving the stack of checks and a deposit slip for $22,500 in the money bag. Amateur or no, they conclude together that either someone was casing the joint, or this was an inside job.

Next, they interview the sister, Mrs. Delgado informs Sara that white people get upset but she, on the other hand, is pissed off. She also tells Warrick that she has insurance on the place. Sara later wonders if Mrs. Delgado's brother might be behind this, and Warrick responds that he doesn't disagree. Moreover, if this is an inside job, not only does the perp get the insurance money, he or she also gets to pocket the cash from the theft. Warrick waves the flyer at Sara and tells her that most people toss flyers on the ground after plucking them from the window. The victim's car's flyer was on the ground. This means that the pamphleteer pinned the flyer on the car shortly before Sante was shot, and may have even been a witness.

And back at the morgue, the coroner is saying that the victim died two to four hours before she was found, but he's still not sure what the cause of death was. Considering the whip and ligature marks, however, he guesses that it may have been violent, and notes that some of the scars on her back are years old; some are fresh. Gil asks whether the marks on the body can be pinned to any cause of death, like violent rape, but David says no—her body indicates she went through a lot of abuse, but not only was it not sexual, she hasn't had sex in months. Gil observes that she's been beaten, but she's got a manicure and pedicure and an expensive boob job. Catherine requests that David extract an implant from the body so they can use its serial number to ID her.

Nicky stops by to visit Greg and learns that the fragment of sticky stuff in the dead woman's wound is a bit of tempered steel with an aluminum coating. Greg suggests she was chained up and also opines that she was wearing liquid latex.

Back at the check cashing murder, Sara is questioning a leaflet passer outer about the night before—did he see anything out of the ordinary? He has little to offer, claiming that most things in Vegas are out of the ordinary.

At the waiting room at a doctor's office, Catherine calls out, "Dr. Cornfeld! Catherine Willows, Las Vegas crime lab." She approaches him and hands him the implant extracted from the body. He is able to look up the patient using the serial number, and tells her the billing address was a third-party place that sends a lot of business, and the recipient of the implant was a Mona Taylor. Catherine gets on her high horse and tells him: "I'll tell you what's a shame. That she was so pretty, and perfect, and still thought she needed implants." Dr. Cornfeld tells her that she shouldn't judge a woman for wanting to improve herself, and invites Catherine to put herself in Mona's shoes. Catherine informs her that she has been in Mona's shoes, and says "Trust me, they were killing me." She then splits, grabs Gil and Brass, and goes to the address given to her by the doctor. .

At a gothic-manor looking place, they climb the stairs. Brass adds that Mona hailed from South Dakota three years ago; he figures she hooked a sugar daddy. Catherine doesn't buy it-- "How much plastic surgery business can one sugar daddy generate?"

A dominatrix opens the door to the room at the top of the stairs and purrs at them, and allows the three to enter. As they enter the foyer, we hear a whip cracking and a man screaming in pain. She asks them if they'd like "individual sessions" or would they prefer to "enjoy each other's submission?" Gil looks uncomfortable; Catherine amused. The dominatrix continues: "You don't have to decide now. Make yourselves comfortable. And welcome to Lady Heather's dominion."

After a commercial break, we find Catherine and Nicky looking at Mona's car. Nicky then goes through the trash, finding several bottles of Wesson, a dull blade, and a stretch of liquid latex. The latex has a watch impression on it; Catherine and Nicky bag it.

Inside the manor, Lady Heather is taking Gil and Brass up a flight of stairs, a chorus of muffled male voices coming from the doors they pass. They hear moans, grunts, and "harder"! Brass casually asks, "Can you tell us what time Mona got off?" Lady Heather tells him "every couple of hours. She enjoyed her work." We then find out that

Mona's last client of the evening was scheduled for 11 PM, and she would have left at midnight.

Soon, Catherine and Nicky come in. Gil sends the two of them back out to begin looking at the pool house; Gil looks at Lady Heather's chamber. He tells her that he thinks her job, and the people who come to her, are deviant, and references the scars and bruises on Mona's back. She responds:" Every job has its peculiar hazards. Rock stars damage their eardrums, football players ruin their knees. In this business, it's scars," She also says that Gil's assumption that Mona's work led to her death is currently only an assumption. He tells her that the whip marks on Mona Taylor were fresh and she is incredulous-- Mona was dominant with her clients, though she did see people off the books. Gil concludes that they may be looking for one of her regular clients.

Meanwhile, Nicky and Catherine are on their way to the pool house, passing a room all dolled up as a school room. They regard it with interest, but pass it, and stop in a bare room where a chain hangs from the ceiling, and paddles and studded whipping devices are on the walls. They find a few chipped links in the chain and liquid latex tucked into a crevice on the wall.

At the check cashing place, Warrick learns that a tire print he lifted off the crime scene matches the car description the leaflet passer-outer gave. Then Sara determines that -- the bullet they dug out of Sante's thigh just happens to be from the same caliber gun the victim owns.

At the morgue, we learn that Mona died from asphyxiation and she had red circular marks on the inside of her nose. Gil asks David if the marks could have been made by something like a straw. David is confused but says they could have been, but what would a straw be for? Gil thinks it could have been used for air.

At the manor, Lady Heather takes Catherine to a storage shed filled with rubber hoses and black masks. Catherine admits that she doesn't have a warrant but Lady Heather invites her to go ahead, and they sort of bond over the fact that Lady Heather tells Catherine she'd make a great dominatrix, and could make $20,000 a month doing so. She declines.

At CSI headquarters, Greg looks at the masks and whips taken from the manor. Gil says he thinks she was a "switch" for her off-the-books clients. If Mona's DNA is in one of these masks, then she was the submissive on the night she died, according to Gil. Greg runs tests and finds DNA, some hers, some belonging to someone else.

Gil and Catherine, in order to get a fix on the killer, start by looking at the watch imprint on the latex and the one from Mona's wrist. The molds are similar and the computer puts together the top mold (from the latex) and the bottom mold (from the wrist) and yields a simulation.

At the case of the check cashing place: Sante says his parents are in a hospital on their death beds. They begin to ask about the gun, and are interrupted as the rest of the Delgado family comes in.

Later, Catherine is at a private residence, asking a gentleman holding a baby about the watch. He denies missing a watch of any sort. The baby sullies his diaper and the husband excuses himself to change it. Catherine stops him to ask if bought a diamond watch at Maarten Jewelers in the Forum. He says no, but Gil then notes that they know someone in the Nelson household bought the watch, since Brass has the receipt. They figure it's his wife.

At the office of his wife, Eileen Nelson's Catherine and Gil are questioning her and she seems not particularly thrilled by taking time off her day to discuss a watch with them. When Gil comments that her office has no pictures, she replies with "I know what they look like." Eileen won't show the watch without a warrant, and then she says that she lost the watch on a business trip. Catherine asks if she lost it when sharing a suite with her boss on a "business trip" she took to California Catherine asks sweetly. Eileen tells her that she's a corporate litigator, and that she won't show them diddly without a warrant, and that they best not come back until they have one.

Back at the check cashing case, Sara and Warrick learned that fiberglass was found on the bag, meaning it got there from the knife used to cut the bag. This particular type of fiberglass has beads of resin that make it harden into a mold. Sara and Warrick check out nearest fiberglass-containing place, and they shortly get an accessory to the crime: Hector, brother-in-law of Sante and husband to Mrs. Delgado. He runs. Warrick catches him. Hector then tells him he borrowed the car from a friend, and they masterminded the robbery.

It's not long before Gil and Catherine re-appear at Eileen's. Less than ecstatic to see them again, she looks at the warrant and spits out: "Is this some kind of joke? This is limited to my watch box." She tells Gil and Catherine that the watch box is in her glove compartment. There is a liquid latex scrap in the box.

At the manor, Gil shows Heather a picture of Cameron and Eileen and asks if she's seen them before. The husband, she says; not the wife. They then proceed to flirt and drink tea.

Back to the B plot: Hector's wife finds out that he's involved and that her brother has been taking from the till, too and demands that they are jailed. And then they are.

Catherine and Gil return and search Cameron's mini-van. Eileen pulls up and threatens to sue them for harassment. Catherine retaliates with: "Played in any sandboxes lately, Mr. Nelson?" Cameron looks up, sheepish.

At the interrogation tank, Eileen has appointed herself to be Cameron's attorney even though he's not really pleased with the idea and accuses her of sleeping with her boss, and goes off on her for being a bad wife and mother. Catherine offers to get him a glass of water. Eileen yells: "No! No water, no gum, no anything. If you think you can trick him into giving some DNA, you're mistaken." Eileen barks. Gil then breaks the news to her that her husband made Mona Taylor wear liquid latex every time he paid to humiliate her. Cameron would put a mask on her face and cover her body in liquid latex. Gil then breaks in to armchair psyche mode: "He made her into nothing, in order to make her into you. Cameron couldn't dominate you, so he dominated Mona. We then see a recreation of the act in grainy flashback, where Cameron is screaming that he wants Eileen to beg for everything, and then suffocates Mona. Eileen counters that if what she heard is what they've got, she's happy to go to trial. Gil says he will match the epithelials when Cameron snaps: "Okay, I have an idea. Why don't we test little Dylan's epithelials, see if his daddy isn't really your law partner? 'Cause God knows you haven't let me touch you in three years. I'm out of here." And he leaves.

Minutes later, Catherine tells Gil that she thinks they have a healthy relationship because she doesn't pour liquid latex on Greg every time he irritates her. Gil furtively looks around and leans in, saying, "Okay. I never told anyone this, Catherine..."

And then the episode ends.

And Then There Were None

At a casino, a man slides a $100 bill across the table to the blackjack table for change. She calls out "Changing one hundred," which is confirmed by the pit boss, and then slides it into the little slots on the table for the big bills. In the next scene, a uniformed security officer comes over with a steel lockbox, then bends over the table, slides out the steel box, and replaces it with a new one. The security guy then looks up at one of the surveillance cameras set in the ceiling and gives it a thumbs-up. At the surveillance office, they see all of this go down on a small monitor. They say: "Section G-3 all clear. En route to H-4 and then soft-count." The camera pulls back to focus on monitor where three people wearing sun glasses are entering the casino.

The three of them spread out on the casino floor, and then the blonde woman takes out a gun and shoots down the chandelier. The one in the curly brown wig and red coat shoots the security guard in the back, then takes the money out of the lock box. The blond continues to cover the other half of the casino floor.

Up in the surveillance booth, one of the men shouts, "Security intercept at section G-5! Contain! Contain!" The three of them then shoot their way out of the casino. The blond shoots the barware, causing panic and loud noises, and the other two shoot security people instead. Just then, one goes down in a convulsion and falls.

Later, Gil and Brass are walking down the stairs. Brass, as usual, apprises us of the situation: "Five guards, three civilians wounded, one dead bad guy, armed robbers snatched the lockboxes from two high-stakes tables right off the rolling cage. Three women -- well armed and well muscled, that got away with $250,000." Gil kneels down by the body of one of the robbers pulls off a wig. It's a man. Brass looks unsettled.

After the commercial break, Brass continues to uphold his obligation to provide exposition: "Same M.O. as Laughlin, men dressed as women, came in and shot the place to hell." Gil thinks that Laughlin was a just dress rehearsal. He and Brass walk toward the floor boss, Mr. Duncan and asks him to tell them what happened. Mr. Duncan says they'd just made money transfer to the rolling cages. Then the chandelier came crashing down so he dropped to his knees, and took cover. They excuse him and discuss what they've learned: Gil opines that the chandelier served to distract the guards, and make them easy targets. Chaos moves in one direction, the money moving in the other. We see another recreation of the crime scene in flashback.

Meanwhile, Sara and Catherine are driving down a stretch of highway at night, towards as small town with a population of twenty people. They pull in to a little Kwik Mart, and a trooper grins and accuses them of getting lost. Sara and Catherine remind him that the body is going to stay dead and can wait twenty hours if need be; it won't go anywhere. The learn that Dustin Bale is the name of the corpse, and he was shot chest. Before he can take off, Sara asks, "Officer Spencer, did you touch anything?" Officer Spencer seems insulted by this suggestion. He apologizes and takes off.

Sara and Catherine enter the convenience store and Catherine notices what looks like mashed potatoes on the floor. A potato, we learn, can act as a silencer. Sara then wanders over to the cash register, and sees that sale was eight hours ago. The assailant must have flipped the sign from "open" to "closed" on the way out, thus making sure no potential customers would come in. Sara notices a security camera, and goes to get the camera down. It's plastic--a Nine-volt attached to a blinking light.

Back at the casino, Gil and Brass are taking down contradictory statements from the witnesses. They break. Brass says, "I've interviewed seventeen people. No two accounts are alike." Gil tells him, "A professor conducted an experiment, asked a bunch of students to count the number of times the ball was passed...during the game, a person dressed in a gorilla suit ran across the court. When the professor asked his students if they noticed the gorilla, fifty percent responded, 'What gorilla?'" Brass doesn't find this helpful. He says, "That's wonderful, Gil. If I see a gorilla, I'll arrest it"

Outside, Nicky examines the get-away car. We establish that the car did not peel out, and that it's beige and beat up. Nicky down and examines a puddle of dark fluid that smells like wood. It seems to be transmission fluid, but it's the wrong color.

At the morgue, David is prying bullets out of the body of the dead would-be casino robber when Gil comes in. We find out that the body is actually one Adam Burrow, shot in the back at close range. Gil deduces that Adam was shot in the back by one of his own partners, since the bullet used is a .45 and not a nine-millimeter.

Back in BFE, is blowing through a long plastic tube, which dispenses a fine white powder over the cardboard sign to get prints. Sara lifts prints off the counter and says to herself "Suspect entered, shoots the clerk through the potato, then hops up and over, leaving behind shoeprints, grabs the cash, flips the sign from open to closed, then exits." Catherine notes that the shoe sprint is relatively small, so they may be looking for a minor.

Meanwhile, Warrick has noticed something on the security cams. He thinks that he knows how it all happened: the boys took out the casino security while the woman in black shot out the chandelier. Shortly after determining they could escape, the one in the brown wig shot Adam. They then turn to the lone woman -- dressed as a woman, among men dressed as women – and Gil lauds it as a good disguise.

At the Kwik E Mart, Catherine gets pissed, picks on Sara for her technique at lifting prints, and asserts loudly that she has earned the right to pick her cases, and expresses outrage that the coroner is four hours late. Sara gets up, puts some change on the counter, and silently hands Catherine an energy bar. Catherine takes it and says, "If I start eating, I will shut up." Sara heads back toward the body and asks Catherine, "Do you have a mirror?" Catherine, who is being pretty bitchy, asks, "Since when do you care about your appearance?" Then she feels bad and adds, "I mean, at a crime scene." Sara explains she wants to examine the body but since she's not allowed to touch it, she wants to use the mirror to help her. Just as Sara's getting ready to do so, coroners come in to fetch the body. Catherine is pleased as punched to see them.

Back at the lab, Greg tells Nicky what the fluid was: type F with Dextron. Nicky explains, "someone put the wrong type of fluid in the car's transmission. See, Ford automobiles use a thick, type-F transmission fluid. General Motors uses a yellow fluid, with Dextron. Now, when Dextron's put into a Ford, it thins that type-F fluid. Friction builds, gears grind. Second gear is usually the first to go. Friction causes the engine to overheat, in turn cooking the transmission fluid, turning it brown. Leak on the pavement is the first clue you've got a problem." Nicky is now looking for leaky Fords with damaged second gears.

Later, Warrick and Brass are about to go through Adam's apartment for clues. Adam had recently exited the pen after spending four-years there for larceny. They are at the apartment to look for anything that links Adam to his robber friends. Warrick instantly zeroes in on the dirty laundry. Brass digs in to Adam's closet, then quips, "While you're at it, don't forget his wigs and bras."

Back at CSI, Sara found a match to the shoe print: Skechers, size 5. They are looking for a female with small feet. The tech then informs them that she and Catherine lifted 82 suspect prints, and the only one they've ID'd comes from the officer who seemed insulted at the suggestion that he'd touch anything. The tech then finds another match on another print -- it's Tammy Felton, the kidnappee-turned-sociopath from last season. Catherine corners Gil and asks, "Do you remember Tammy Felton?" and lets him in on the fact that Tammy is a prime suspect in the Kwik-E-Mart homicide. Just then, Greg interrupts by calling for Grissom; he hauls Catherine with him as he goes.

Greg tells him that ballistics sent up one of the .45 bullets found on the scene, and it had potato on it. Gil notes that his case had three robbers, and even with one dead and one Tammy, they're still one suspect short. Just then, Sara comes in and tells them she found: Darin Hanson, the man that Tammy met after jumping bail. Ballistics then informs them that the bullets from the casino match those at the convenience store. Nicky then drops by and tells them that they may have found the getaway car—a beige 1977 Mercury Cougar.

They go to the car together. Nicky notices a dirt bike at the scene and checks it out, while Gil and Catherine pop the trunk. Tammy Felton's inside, dead, and her blonde wig is in the trunk with her.

David checks her out at the morgue. He confirms that she didn't put up much of a fight, and that there are contusions on the neck, and cartilaginous tracheal rings are crushed. Catherine flashes to a scene of Darin kissing Tammy shortly before strangling her. David swabbed Tammy's neck and found epithelials; he's going to test them against Darin Hanson's DNA.

Later, Nicky climbs out of the Cougar and has found some of the same dust found on Adam's body. Greg says it's silica dust, and each particle's a hundred times smaller than a grain of sand. Gil comes in and tells them that silica is used to make class and mined in open pits. Why?" Gil replies. Nicky tells him that silica was found both on Adam Brower's clothing and the getaway vehicle, and Gil notes that there's an abandoned silica mine not too far from the convenience store.

Gil, Nicky, Warren, and random LVPD guys appear at the mine to check it out. Gil immediately hones in on a motorcycle parked next to an outhouse. As the three men walk toward the outhouse, the ground glimmers in the beams of their flashlights. They open the outhouse and Darin Hanson's corpse falls out. Warrick notes that Darin's been shot execution-style with a .45.

Later, the team talks through what happened: shortly before pulling off the heist, Tammy and Darin killed the clerk at the convenience store. Then they went to the casino heist, where Darin killed Adam Brower and others. Not much later, Darin killed Tammy, but who killed him, and where's the money? Warrick, who has been on the phone with Laughlin CSI, says that in that heist, there were four robbers, not three. Warrick points out that Mr. Duncan ducked before Tammy shot down the chandelier. In other words, he knew it was coming. They play the security tape slowly until they ascertain that he did, indeed, preemptively take cover. Warrick, by the way, also found out that Duncan was a relatively recent employee, and he had last worked in Laughlin, at the practice casino.

Gil and Catherine catch Duncan on his way out of town and take him to the station and interrogate him. Catherine clarifies that he ducked before anyone had a cause to; he says he saw a gun, so he hit the ground. She also tells him that his car was covered in silica which places him at the scene of Darrin's murder. Duncan protests that Darin was already dead by the time he got to the site. He then admits he helped him out and told him when and where to hit. Catherine points out that it still doesn't explain why Duncan went to see Darin. Duncan continues to ignore his lawyer and says he went with the intention of collecting his share but the money was gone, Darin was dead, he panicked. Brass lets him in on the fact that when someone is killed during the commission of a felony, all the co-conspirators are liable; Duncan's lawyer says, "Let's make a deal." "Darin was the only one I spoke to -- I never even met the other three!" Duncan protests.

A lab tech has obtained the surveillance video from Laughlin. The fourth crook is Dustin Bale, the clerk from the convenience store. Sara thinks Darin killed him first. They cleared out the register to make it look like a robbery. Gil says, however, "The pit boss said there was Darin plus three." "Because he knew there were four at the Laughlin heist," Sara adds. Gil points out that it would have been difficult for Duncan to see how many people were there when he was ducking and hiding on the floor, and they still don't know who killed Hanson. Sara says. Meanwhile, Catherine and Nicky look at the bullet from Darin's head. It's a .45 automatic fired from a polygonal barrel, probably a Heckler and Koch. Of the eighteen registered in-state, one belongs to Officer Spencer.

At a highway patrol office, Officer Spencer is asking if they're really accusing him of murder. Catherine asks where the cash is. He says: "I'm a state trooper," Spencer replies. Catherine hypothesizes that Spencer caught Tammy and Darin knocking off the convenience store, and Tammy talked him into letting them go. Spencer took a wad of cash and killed Darin while he was taking a potty break in an outhouse. Gil and Catherine confirm this by seeing that the silica blanketing the carpet and leads to Spencer's locker. The CSIs then easily find the money stashed beneath a false bottom in Spencer's locker.

Catherine is incredulous that $250,000 made a career cop a rogue. Gil counters, "Well, he had his price." "We all do," Catherine says.

Elli

On the strip near the MGM grand, young dark-haired guy is trying to get the attention of passersby. A Palm-Beach-old-money yuppy-looking man and woman notice the nervous tourist and head toward him, looking concerned.

The tourist explains that he has ten thousand dollars in chips, and is barred, and can't get cashed out as a result. He then asks that the couple take his chips into the casino and cash them for him. But. He wants a guarantee that they'll come back with his money; a simple $2000 would do, and then he'll return all that, plus $1000. The couple agrees.

In the next scene, we see cashier looking at the chips and saying that the chips can't be cashed. They're fake. They run to find the man who gypped them, and as they stand in the doorway of the Tropicana's parking structure, they hear the squeal of tires.

And of course, in the next scene, the garage is decorated with yellow police tape, and Brass plays narrator as he and Gil arrive on the scene. "The guy was running one of the oldest scams in Vegas. Would have gotten away with it too, 'til the getaway driver put a nickel in the guy's jukebox.

Those are the Ortons, from Florida. They ID'd the deceased as the con man." The con man is dead on the floor and surrounded by hundred dollar bills. Apparently, there's no surveillance in the garage. Sam Vega, detective, hands a plastic bag full of poker chips to Brass.

After we return from these special messages, we see Gil in the halls of CSI. He walks briskly, pausing to lecture Greg that he shouldn't listen to Black Flag at work, and then continues down the hall and bumps into Catherine. He shows her a jar of bugs and introduces them hissing roaches from Madagascar. They are capable of running two and a half miles per hour and Gil is going to race them at the fifth annual entomological convention in Duluth. Vaguely amused, Catherine asks Gil who will be supervising the night shift—she will be on a plane to Reno as Sam's date for a new casino opening.

Gil asks Warrick and at first, he's surprised and suggests that his colleagues take charge, but then agrees reluctantly. Gil takes off to go to his bug soiree.

Nicky and Sara, meanwhile, are doing all kinds of evidence analysis to a soundtrack of eurotrash downtempo, when Warrick stops by and bosses them around. No one has been told that there's a new sheriff in town, so at first, Sara refuses to do his bidding and then eventually resentfully gives in. Nick acts like a snot and walks away.

Warrick then heads into the morgue, where David is examining one Vincent Avery, killed by a gunshot wound to the left ear as he got into a car. Warrick concludes that the victim knew the killer and then looks through the x-rays and sees that something is in the victim's stomach. Indeed, there are a series of small white sacs, like cycsts almost, against the stomach lining, surrounded by green slime. They are not cysts. They are, in actuality, fifty balloons containing a schedule one substance, washed down with lime Jello. Warrick wonders why a drug mule would bother with the chip trick.

Brass then pops in to tell us all about Mr. Avery, a petty, low-rent con man out of Atlantic City . Nicky, hard at work on the tire treads, points to an anomaly in the tread and asks Brass if he thinks it could be a nail embedded in the tire. He has no strong opinion.

Sara stops by the lab to see what Greg has come up with after analyzing his personal effects. The pills he had on them were charcoal. If he didn't chase the balloons with charcoal, a bite of an ordinary chocolate bar would change the acidity in his stomach and possibly eat away the balloon, so he'd overdose. Not only that, but Sara has found plane tickets in Avery's shirt. He was in seat 4-A and an Ellie Rebecca was in seat 4-B.

Warrick dusts the plane ticket stubs for prints and up pops the name Ellie Rebecca Brass. Warrick has the bad news of telling Brass that his daughter is implicated in the homicide. The two men confirm that someone from LVPD will have to bring in Ellie, and Brass will be unable to be on case for obvious personal reasons.

In the next scene, Vega escorts Ellie into the interrogation room. Ellie sees him and grins. She heads down the hall to greet her father spits on his badge. Brass, unmoved by her performance, asks placidly "So we're going to pick up right where we left off?"

Elsewhere in the catacombs of the CSI office, Sara is going through the hundred dollar bills, documenting their serial numbers. Something odd catches her eye. She asks the lab tech if he knows what the intaglio script is, and indeed he does: it's the engraving on Ben Franklin's collar. Sara points out that she can't find the intaglio script on this one bill; the lab tech can't either.

Meanwhile, Ellie flips through photos of Avery's dead body and says in the voice of a bored post-adolescent: "Everyone I sleep with dies." She then digs into her purse for cigarettes and asks, "Mind if I smoke?", and a false casino chip falls out.

Warrick asks Ellie: "So. You two fly to Baja, pose as a married couple, bring home a stomach-load of blow, and then run chip scams? Who's taking your drug profits?" She denies having any idea what he's talking about in her bored snotty teenager voice. He asks her where she was during Avery's shooting; she tells him she was home in the bathroom. They opine that she was indeed in the bathroom crapping out balloons filled with cocaine. Warrick tells Ellie that they'd like her to agree to X rays and she acquiesces. Vega says he'd like to see her car but Ellie lent it to her boyfriend. Ellie informs Warrick that he looks like Lenny Kravitz and she normally doesn't like African Americans but she'll make an exception for him. He ignores her, and asks her the name of her boyfriend. Finally, she tells him: Keith Driscoll.

Sara is still examines the fake looking bill, comparing it to a real one. On a real hundred-dollar bill, the words "the United States of America" are engraved on the border of Ben's portrait. Sara asks lab tech Ronnie about pigmentation as Treasury seals and serial numbers should be the same color. Ronnie also tells her that no copier or printer on the market can hold a true green. Yellow and blue hues always bleed in. Sara then considers notifying the Secret Service about the fraudulent Benjamins.

Meanwhile, Ellie's X-ray shows that she is not carrying any balloons of cocaine in her stomach. He asks if she realizes the overdose risk she runs every time she ingests a pellet. She says that there is only a risk if she eats, and she just makes a dirty joke about eating Warrick.

Elsewhere, Brass is driving and simultaneously looking up Ellie's car registration when his cell rings. It's Catherine, warning him not to go it alone if he finds the boyfriend. Too late-the boyfriend's car is sharing the road with Brass. He pursues the car, pulls it over, kicks out a hapless hitchhiker, pulls Driscoll out, pins him to the car, and asks him what he is doing to his daughter. Driscoll claims that Ellie turned him on to coke so he could carry for her. Lucky for Driscoll, back up black and whites appear and Driscoll is taken in.

At the next scene, Would Be Good Samaritan from Florida Mr. Orton is asking Sara why he can't have his money back. Sara explains that it's counterfeit, and she's obligated to take it out of circulation. Mr. Orton doesn't look too shocked. He explains that a gas station attention told him one of his hundreds were phony, so then he went to the bank to turn in the bad money for some real money, but couldn't. Sara reminds him of a little law called Title 18, Section 473 of the United States Code, making it punishable by up to fifteen years, for knowingly passing on bad money." They don't look pleased. She then tells them that a special agent from Secret Service will want to talk to them about a deposition.

In the next scene, Special Agent Beckman from the Treasury Department meets with Warrick and informs him that their lab will want to analyze that money too. Warrick has no idea what he's talking about. Just then, Sara comes over and introduces herself to Beckman. Nicky swings by, Warrick and Sara excuse themselves to argue, and after a heated discussion, Sara is dispatched on an errand.

Later, Nicky is happy that the treads from the crime scene match the treads on the car. Warrick then sums up the evidence again for Driscoll and his lawyer; the meeting ends after the lawyer informs them that Brass pulled a gun on her client. Warrick is clearly stressed out by this development.

Meanwhile, Beckman discusses the counterfeit case with Sara. She shows him a stack of counterfeit bills with different serial numbers, concluding that the couple didn't make just one bill and run off a hundred copies with the same serial number. They burnt separate plates for each serial number. Beckman then informs her "The Duffys are major counterfeiters." –apparently, after getting off the phone with Sara, Beckman opened up a database and learned that the Ortons were the Duffys, who have each done time for interstate fraud and high-end counterfeiting. He tells her he is now going to take his leave to bust the counterfeiting rings and she is clearly yearning to accompany him.

Meanwhile, Warrick tells Brass that they placed Ellie's car at the murder scene, and will be pressing charges against Ellie. They cannot charge Driscoll since Brass put a gun to his head when he pulled him over. Brass asks if they're under the impression that Ellie might perhaps tell the truth rather than do hard time to cover for her boyfriend's murder. Warrick is silent.

Night falls. Warrick is in Gil's office when Grissom's phone rings. He answers. It's Vega, appraising him of an officer involved shooting. Warrick bolts to the scene. The "scene" is a tract home. Brass is sitting on a low wall in the front yard. EMTs wheel out a corpse on a gurney. Surprise surprise: Driscoll has been shot. In the throat. Yuck. Vega tells Warrick: "First officer here found Brass on the floor, woozy. Keith Driscoll, lights out." Ellie is nowhere to be found, and the weapon is missing a round.

Brass tells Vega that he went over to the apartment to look for Ellie on a personal visit. Driscoll was there. They Exchanged Words. Then someone knocked him out. Brass does not remember drawing his gun.

Warrick is cleaning the gun when he finds the shooter's blood on the back of the grip. Nicky leans in and says: "Novice shooters get their hands pinched in the slide." In the next scene, he asks Brass to show him his hands, then asks Brass for his badge.

Beckman, seeing Sara's interest in busting a counterfeiting ring, has asked her to come with him on the bust. She asks sweetly, "Mr. Duffy, can Agent Beckman and I see your burn plates, please?" They have press, ink, burn plates, and paper, but no money. "There is no money," Mrs. Duffy says. Beckman then tells her that the entire situation was a test to see if flawed enforcement personnel would even detect the money in the first place, much less report it. The Duffys (in actuality undercover agents) put bait money in the hands of bad people. Sara reminds them that Avery was killed. Beckman tells Sara she should be proud. She isn't.

In the lab, Greg has sequenced the DNA in the saliva sample off Brass's badge, and the DNA from a Brass blood sample. They are nothing alike. Bass and his alleged daughter have no markers in common. He isn't the father.

Warrick then notes that the plane tickets for Avery and Ellie are charged to the same card as for one Marty Gilmore. In our next seen, Brass and Warrick drive very quickly, and get out of the car to flag down Marty shortly before he takes off in a helicopter. Marty, as it turns out, is the hitchhiker. Warrick turns over Gilmore's hand and notes the pinch. We learn that he shot Driscoll with Brass' gun, and that he set up Ellie for shooting Avery at the casino. Gilmore then doubles over and claims he took a laxative. He too is a drug mule and a balloon must have broken.

Next scene: Brass is given back his badge and told that he only had to surrender it so they could get Ellie's DNA from it. Brass smiles. He then confirms that he already knew that Ellie was not his biological daughter. Then he has a tearful scene where he tries to reunite with his snotty, non-biological daughter.

Gil then arrives with a garment bag and roaches. He reveals that his roaches didn't do well, and asked Warrick how it was to be the King of the Hill while he was gone. He sighs, and tells Grissom what he missed.

Organ Grinder

In the lobby of one of the fancier, more upscale casinos, a young blond man is walking a young blonde woman over to the elevator and telling her that she will just feel right at home in his room. She is quick to inform him: "I don't usually do this. Especially with guys I just met." He reassures her by saying "you can trust me" and they begin making out. She makes a bizarre noise and then points out the corpse on the elevator floor.

In the next scene Gil and Sara enter the crime scene. Brass tells us of an anonymous phone call to 911 immediately before the body's discovery in the elevator. He says that since the man was unconscious but breathing, paramedics took him to Desert Palms hospital, and his name is Bob Fairmont, an upscale home developer. Sara notes that the suit on the man is rumpled. Gil says that it's impossible to redress an unconscious person and make it look like they dressed themselves.

Nicky and Catherine have showed up and have learned that Fairmont was staying in Room 2927. Nicky goes with Catherine to the elevator, and Gil will look at the hotel room with Sara.

Meanwhile, at Desert Palms, Brass is quizzing the widow Fairmont. She notes sadly, "He usually goes with women who look a lot like me, only younger. And I'm embarrassed to admit I've been flattered at times." Brass has formed two theories: the Widow Fairmont has plenty of motivation to see her cheating heartthrob dead, or one of Fairmont's many girlfriends on the side did it. We later learn btw that her husband is in surgery because his organs are being harvested.

In the room, Sara notes that they had champagne, there was no lipstick on either glass, and 911 did say it was a man's voice that placed the call. Gil tells her that the room smells like sex even though the drapes were open. Sara then hones in on a bra.

In the elevator, Nicky and Catherine are looking at some white specks in the carpet and lifts it with tape. She and Nicky then rejoin Sara and Gil in the hotel room, and they spray luminol. Nicky hits the lights. The bed is covered with champagne and semen, and there are semen stains all over the wall. There is a condom on a light fixture. As Gil is leaving, he says, "Oh, and Sara? Last hotel room nearest the stairwell. Easy entry and egress for an intruder, and if a victim fights back, fifty percent less chance of being heard." And now they know what Catherine meant by her "murder central" comment earlier.

At the lab, Greg is given the white sample to analyze. Catherine leaves the lab and runs into Warrick, who tells her that he went to the Fairmont house on one of his first CSI calls three years ago. The man had accidentally shot himself while cleaning his gun. Now made suspicious by this latest turn of events, he runs off to dig up the file and take another look at it. Catherine heads off to Desert Palms hospital to pick up Fairmont's clothes.

Brass and Gil discuss the fact that the 911 tape was lost, and the voice was not actually male but gender indeterminate. Gil goes to visit the coroner. Fairmont died of an apparent aneurysm from what appeared to be a genetic predisposition. Other than that, Fairmont was healthy and also he was an organ donor. The doctors took eight organs in under two hours.

Greg, who has developed a crush on Sara, is swabbing out the condom while trying to ask Sara to have lunch with him. She agrees absentmindedly. Greg then points out that he wants a DNA sample from Fairmont to compare the two, and then Sara puts down the autopsy photos to say "What the heck? Stripes!" and run out of the lab.

.

What she meant was fingernail stripes: horizontal white bands ribbing the nails, possibly indicative of heavy metal poisoning. Gil reminds her that they really can't count on a photo and needs the body, but David released it since he figured that the man died of natural causes. They hunt him down to figure out the name of the mortuary.

When they arrive, the undertaker (who we may remember from episodes past) shows Sara and Nick over to the crematorium where Farimont is being scorched and they learn that Fairmont's wife approved the cremation. Stubborn, Sara takes a chunk of the charred remains and begins to grind it with a mortar and pestle.
Meanwhile, Brass is questioning the Widow Fairmont. He reminds her that when he visited her at the hospital, she told him that her husband was in surgery. He was—Brass assumed he was in surgery to save his life. But he was getting his organs taken.

The widow demands to know why he's being hostile and Brass tells her that it's because her husband was poisoned. Sara explains that heavy metals' heat-resistant properties guarantee that they show up even after cremation, and she found selenium in Fairmont's remains. She also says that people suffering from extra selenium will excrete dimethyl selenide, which smells like garlic. Did her husband smell like garlic? Or have weird lines on his fingernails? She then admits that they didn't spend much time together. Sara asks if that bothered her and she says "I think it would bother any woman." Sara then decides to play a little trivia game and asks her: "Did you know the most common choice of murder among women is poison?" The widow gets extremely upset at the accusation and begins to storm out, saying she only cremated him because it was his wish, not to hide anything, and she had to go now. As leaves, Sara calls out, "Do you want us to notify you?" "Of what?" the Widow inquires. "Of how much selenium your husband was dosed with, over what period of time," Sara replies. "I thought you couldn't tell," she says. Sara says that they can hunt down his organs, and the widow says sure, give her a ring and let her know what they found.

In the next scene, Nicky is talking to a man and a doctor as he explains that his new kidney is poisoned. The man is outraged. He demands to know how this could happen. The doctor tells him that something like this happens so rarely, it isn't tested for. The patient laughs nervously, and Nicky explains why he's in the room; he'd like a biopsy of the kidney but the man refuses. He says it's HIS kidney now. Nicky takes it pretty well. As he leaves, he then compliments the patient on his watch, which is strapped to the hospital bed rail. The patient notes that it died while he was in surgery and now the hands are stuck at eleven o'clock.

Later, we learn that the only person who consented to a biopsy was the heart recipient, which is useless because it doesn't "have a memory for poison", says Gil. Sara starts to ask why they can't just biopsy people without their permission and then is cowed when Gil give her a look that reminds her of probable cause, warrants, and privacy concerns.

In a hospital lab, a woman identifying herself as Claudia Gideon -- secretary to the late Mr. Fairmont -- is there to pick up Fairmont's stuff. Catherine, as it turns out, has already taken it upon herself to pick up his stuff. She explains that the property is now part of an investigation, so she has to take it. Claudia doesn't seem too upset about this development. Catherine takes this opportunity to ask whether Claudia was around three years ago when Fairmont shot himself while cleaning his gun. No dice-- Claudia was out sick that day.

So it isn't long before Claudia finds herself in the interrogation room. Brass and Gil learn quickly that Claudia may not have been in the hotel room with Fairmont, but she's the one who dressed him and placed him in the elevator. She claimed she went to the hotel on business, found Fairmont naked and unconscious, and dressed him. She then, as a matter or fact, did go down a stairwell after doing so and would be just pleased as punch to give them a DNA sample to compare with what's on the condom. Warrick then appears to remind us that Fairmont shot himself in the leg three years ago -- and why wasn't that scar noted during the autopsy? Warrick, more experienced that he was three years ago, has realized that Fairmont did not shoot himself in the thigh while cleaning his gun. Someone was most likely sitting in a chair, aiming for his groin as he came in the door. Claudia says, "I didn't shoot him."

In the next scene, Fairmont's widow admits that she shot her husband because she caught him cheated. She claims she wanted to report it but her husband, a fan of reputation over health, vetoed it. Warrick mentions that he's taking the case to the DA even though it's three years old.

In the next scene, Gil and Catherine break it down. Claudia has dandruff and the main ingredient in dandruff medicines: selenium sulfide. And indeed, when they go through Claudia's office they find a big bottle of prescription shampoo. At that moment, Claudia arrives from dinner. Brass and Catherine ask her why shampoo is in her office, specifically, shampoo full of the same poison found in Bob Fairmont's remains.

The widow, who, for some reason is present as they go through Claudia's office, almost slaps the secretary and they fight over why he had a mistress until Brass breaks it up.

The poor kidney recipient then tells Nicky he'll do the biopsy since his body is rejecting it anyway, and elects to give up the kidney.

Sara then interrupts Nicky and Gil when Nicky is relating this information. She tells them that the prints in the shampoo bottle prove Fairmont was in the suite with her husband.

They haul her back in for questioning. She apparently didn't tell them she was in the suite with him because, well, gosh, they didn't ask. Brass asks when she realized that he had an aneurysm and she protests, saying she's not a doctor. Brass tells her he tested the champagne bottle for selenium and she says, softly, "I didn't think poison caused strokes."

Gil goes back to looking at Fairmont's ashes. Three gold crowns are missing because his wife had them removed prior to cremation. Outside in the parking lot Nicky happens to notice the widow swoon and faint. He catches her, and then calls an ambulance. At the hospital, she is treated with a shot of hydropazine -- used to counteract heavy metal poisoning – discharged.

So now Claudia is back for questioning. She claims that Mrs. Fairmont poisoned herself, and/or is trying to frame her for killing him. She also points out that Fairmont took his gold teeth and what kind of person would do that?

Mrs. Fairmont counters that she had his watch and ring removed too. She doesn't care how it looks, she has nothing to hide. Brass asks what Claudia might have against them, and she points out that her husband refused to leave her for Claudia.

Claudia refutes this. Brass is confused.

Greg then saves the day by giving this information to Sara after performing an exhaustive search of public records: ten years ago, Claudia was married to a rich Arizona rancher and Mrs. Fairmont happened to be the rancher's secretary. The rancher died young; Claudia donated his organs and cremated his body. The liver recipient died two months later, and now Nicky and Sara have an excuse to go to Arizona.

Nicky and Sara watch as the poor liver recipient's grave is being exhumed. They then take the liver to test for poison, and find that it contains sodium selinite.

Claudia says, "We have never represented that we didn't know each other previously". Catherine says she thinks she knows what happened: Claudia poisoned her husband and

Mrs. Fairmont caught her and got Claudia to splitting the estate with her in exchange for keeping quiet. They ran out of money and moved to repeat the crime with another rich man. Then things got sticky Mrs. Fairmont actually fell in love with her husband. No matter; the DA, after reviewing evidence and meeting with Mrs. Fairmont's lawyers, has decided not to move forward and press charges. A she-said-he-said case, after all, usually yields deadlock.

Out the widows go, and Sara, predictably, is pissed. She asks Gil:, "What are we doing? Digging up graves, chasing prints...if it's no good in court, if the killers win." Gil says it's not about win or lose, and that if Sara gets mad, the criminals win. The good news, however, is that there's no statute of limitation on murder.

You've Got Male

Somewhere that is supposed to be on the outside of Vegas but looks much too green, a woman is riding her horse. She dismounts because he horse is beginning to spook at the site of a corrugated metal cylinder, and sees that there is a dead body in the pipe

By the time Gil et al arrives, night has fallen. He, this time, provides exposition: "A girl in a culvert pipe at a highway construction site in the middle of an alfalfa field." Brass adds that a road crew took off at 3:30 and the body was discovered at 5:15. Sara walks towards him and tells him that she has found a second body.

David the coroner tells use that both women died approximately 12 hours ago. The brunette has an injury to the cervical spine that seems to be "hands-on". Gil and David agree that yes, someone snapped the brunette's neck, and yes, she died instantly. The blonde, on the other hand, had cut glass embedded in many wounds all over her body, and fingernail mark looking scratches on her neck. Cause of death: severed brachial artery. Then they show it. Gil points at the brunette and extrapolates from her dyed hair, tattoos, and piercings that she wanted attention. The blonde, however, doesn't even have pierced ears and didn't shave her legs.

Nicky and Catherine have wandered from the desert to this oddly lush. Nicky notices that the bullet went straight through the now- dead hunter . Nicky picks up the hunting rifle and comments that it is a Winchester 70. The mobile coroner arrives and sticks a thermometer in the wound so he can estimate time of death. We see the entire process. Nicky notes that all of the bullets for the gun are accounted for and the rifle was never fired.

Catherine is snapping photos and the coroner advises her that the man died at 2 PM. Catherine then fishes a wallet from his pants. The man is one James Jasper of Las Vegas, NV. Catherine muses that a hunter shot at a deer and missed. The bullet kept going until it hit the now-dead man, who, it should be noted, was not in his orange safety gear.

Meanwhile, the brunette has been identified. She is Joan Marks, felony shoplifter. Warrick has been sent with a warrant to check out the address.

Back in the hunting grounds, Nicky sees a bullet embedded in a tree trunk and calls Catherine over to look at it. He is puzzled as to how to extract it without damaging it and calls Catherine over to get her input.

Day breaks. Sara and Gil are walking up the driveway of a suburban Vegas home. They enter the garage, and Sara gets behind the wheel of the car stowed within. It's an older car, with only 1200 miles on it, registered to a Donna Marks. Warrick pops in and tells them that Donna is the blonde corpse, and Joan's sister. Warrick also reveals that the house used to belong to Donna and Joan's late mother, and Donna's been living in it alone since her mother died. Joan lived in Henderson.

Out back, on the patio, they observe a melee of shattered patio-door glass and a few numbered cones. Warrick also points out the bloody imprints he's found and logged. Sara found blood on Joan's shoe, so if the blood matches up, that places her at the house. If she stepped in Donna's blood, Joan must have been ok enough to be walking around while Donna lay bleeding and injured or possibly dead. Gil walks over to the fridge and surveys the take-out menu collection. Its contents are limited to a collection of take-out containers.

Gil and Sara ascertain that the family-sized portions of sweet-and-sour pork in the front are still fresh, but the single-sized portions in the have gone bad. Her home office

is filled with expensive electronic equipment and masses of
mail order catalogues. These catalogs, the takeout, and the
1200 miles on her indicate to Gil that she may be
agoraphobic. Sara says she'll nab Donna's computer, go
through her email, and see what she finds. She then heads
to the bathroom, and noticing that the toilet seat is up, tells
Gil that a man must have been there.

When Catherine arrives at CSI, Nicky tells her that the
coroner said that James Jasper died because the bullet
severed an abdominal artery, and he bled out. Catherine
and Nick go to the widow to talk to her. She is
appropriately dismayed and tells them that her husband
left early, and when he failed to appear before dinner, she
assumed he had bagged a deer. He was able to hunt on the
weekday because the two of them had both been laid off
recently—James handled it well until they had to ask her
parents for help with the rent. Catherine asks if James was
an experienced hunter; he was. Mrs. Jasper breaks down
again and starts sobbing. She barely manages to tell Nick
that James was usually very safety conscious, so not
wearing a vest doesn't sound like something he'd do.

Meanwhile, stops by the lab to pick up the DNA samples
re: the scratches on Donna's neck. He is somewhat thrown
off when he is told that the scratches were inflicted by her
sister. In the hall, Sara and Brass tell each other what

they've learned: Joan Marks and her boyfriend Gavin Pallard had restraining orders against each other.

They immediately pay him a visit. He points to a scar on his cheek and says that Joan threw furniture at him and had a bad temper. Gavin says that despite the restraining order, Joan came back over to his house three times because he's just that good. Sara He says that the morning before, she threw a coffee pot at him and got lost. Joan took his T-Bird when she left, and he'd like his car back. Sara ask if she had said that she was going to her sister's house but he scoffs at the suggestion. Joan her sister did not get along at all. Sara asks Gavin to see the soles of his shoes.

In the ballistics lab, Nicky learns to his disappointment that the end of the bullet he dug out of the tree is discolored, which indicates oxidation. So the bullet has been there awhile. He brightens somewhat when Vega shows him and Catherine a two-month-old insurance policy for two million dollars for James Jasper, with his wife as the beneficiary.

Meanwhile, down in the basement, Warrick is piecing together glass from Donna's house.

Meanwhile, Sara and Gil are going through Donna's computer. Apparently her ISP is called "Internet Online." Anyway, they learn that Donna was a telecommuter. She mail ordered stuff from catalogues via the phone and received confirmations via email. Donna spent time in chat rooms -- she was involved in book clubs and collected fountain pens. There was only one buddy on the internet buddy list with the screen name Apollo." Gil and Sara pull up the log of their most recent chat, and Sara begins reading: "'I know it sounds weird, but my life began when I first heard your voice. When you said my name, it felt so right. Did you feel it too? It's easy to wear your heart on your sleeve when you're not looking in his eyes." They track down Apollo's IP address -- Western Nevada Correctional Facility, 23000 Ganza Avenue, Ely, Nevada.

So of course, they pay a visit to the prison. This prison is special: it's privately owned and is like a theme park or a cross between summer camp and traffic school. Gil meets with the warden and he takes him to a room where inmates are working at terminals handling mail-order business. The prison's several contracts with retailers are all perfectly legal. Gil gets around to asking about Apollo, and it turns out that his real name is Mickey Rutledge, and he was released three days ago.

At CSI, Warrick flags Sara down to show her a fiber picked from Joan's clothing. Warrick guesses it came from car upholstery. Gavin's car is blue with black upholstery. Brass and Sara then pay a visit to Gavin about his whereabouts on the night of the murders. Gavin's lawyer says, "My client went there after the fact. He was looking for his girlfriend. He didn't find her." Brass and Sara note that Gavin did, however, "forget" to call 911 after seeing a pool of blood and broken glass.

Back in the great outdoors, Nicky and Catherine are searching for a bullet in a forest. This is as tedious and formidable as it sounds. They do, however, learn that James Jasper didn't buy a hunting license. Catherine notes that she hasn't heard a single shot all day, and the park ranger tells her that most hunters come around at dusk, or dawn, but Jasper died around 2 PM.

Gil comes back from the prison and finds that the finger prints on the toilet seat from Donna's house have been processed. The prints belong to Mickey / Apollo. Mickey is currently in custody.

They haul him in for questioning. At first he says he wasn't at her house, and then breaks down and admits that she invited him over. He brought her flowers and they had take out.. Mickey says Joan came over and picked a fight with

Donna. He does admit to coming over and using the toilet, however, he does not admit to murder. He is let go and the parole officer promises to keep a watchful eye on him.

Gil checks up on how Warrick is doing with piecing the glass together. He has a point of impact, roughly sixty-five inches from the base. Donna is 5'6 so it almost seems like she was upright when the glass broke—almost like she walked right through the door. Sara drops by to tell them they found Gavin's car five miles from the dump site. The first thing they notice is that the radiator is cracked. This time, however, it was filled up with water instead of coolant.

At the morgue, Nicky and Catherine have found gunshot residue on Jasper's shirt, indicating that he was shot at close range. Murder or suicide? There's no evidence of a murder, nor a struggle. They leave the morgue to check out widow James' alibi, and on the way out, run into Sara, who is frustrated with the challenges she has faced in trying to lift a print from the radiator cap. Greg has had more luck; his analysis of the coolant is that it contains potassium, and phosphorus.

At the other plot, Mrs. Jasper's alibi checks out. She was at work and ate at her desk. Neither think he was hit by a professional, since a pro would have shot him in the head or spine. Nicky points out that abdominal wounds take time to bleed out. It would have taken at least ten minutes for hemorrhagic shock to set in and in the meantime, he would have been able to walk around. Maybe he had a second weapon that he shot himself with and hid? They don waders and search the pond near the place where Jasper was found. Eventually, with hard work and stick-to-it-iveness, Catherine and Nicky find a gun. They theorize that Jasper shot himself, threw the pistol into the pond, and staggered back against a tree, trying to make it look like an accidental death so his wife could collect on the insurance.

They now have to tell her that she doesn't get the insurance money. Catherine begins by telling Mrs. Jasper that she had purchased a life insurance policy in which she was the sole beneficiary but Mrs. Jasper has no idea what she's talking about. Catherine explains that her husband staged his own death to look like a homicide. As a beneficiary, if she knew of his intentions to take his own life, that would constitute fraud. She starts crying and said that if she knew, she would have stopped him—she had no idea about the policy. As it turns out, James forged his wife's signature, and opened the insurance account in his wife's name. Then he planned how to kill himself in a way to make it look like it was not a suicide so his wife could collect the money. This hits Mrs. Jasper like a ton of bricks and she begins to sob again.

Gil, meanwhile, has returned to alfalfa country, where learns that the farmer uses nitrogen, phosphorous, potassium on his crops, and takes prints from the spigot.

Back at the interrogation tank with Mickey, Gil theorizes aloud about how it all went down. Joan came over, and ordered Mickey to get out because he was an ex con. The two sisters fought. Donna was killed by mistake. Joan then told Mickey that she would make sure he took the rap, and Mickey sprung on her and broke her neck. He then used the T-Bird to hide and transport the bodies, but the radiator gave out, so he filled it with the water from the alfalfa farm. Mickey tries to explain why he didn't just let Joan make the call and plead his innocence. He says: "I would have landed myself right back in the joint...who's going to believe a guy like me?" "A guy like me," Gil says.

Identity Crisis

A man listening to bad pop country drives on a twisty, rural road on the outskirts of Vegas. He pulls over to pick up a man holding a sign that reads Vegas. The hitchhiker slides into the car and the driver asks, "So where are you headed?" The hooded man turns, and we see that it's Paul Millander. He responds slowly, "It's not where I'm headed..."

In another improbably woody and lush setting, Catherine and Gil get out of a car and walk towards an official type person in a Edgar Hoover style trench coat. He says, "Welcome to Good Springs." The official continues, "I know it's out of your jurisdiction, but it is your name on the tape." He gives them the victim's wallet and they identify the driver of the car that picked up the hitchhiker. It's Pete Walker of California, born August 17, 1957. We see Walker in a tub, shot in the sternum, with a small tape recorder on the tub's edge. Catherine explains to those who may not have seen any of season one: "The M.O.'s the same. Kills men with the same birthday as the anniversary of his father's murder." In Brass' absence, Gil helps her with exposition: "In descending order. First victim was August 17, 1959. Second victim, August 17, 1958. 1957..." They play the tape, and surprise surprise it says: "My name is Pete

Walker. I reside at 715 Lady del Sol and I'm 44 years of age. I'm going to kill myself. I'd like to say 'I love you' to my mother. I'm so sorry. I never wanted to put you through this. I just can't do it anymore..." Walker's voice trails off, and we hear a gunshot. After a moment of silence, Millander's voice wafts from the speakers of the small tape recorder and says: "Happy birthday, Mr. Grissom." Gil's birthday, we learn here, is August 17, 1956.

Gil is taking prints when Nicky and Warrick ask Gil if it's really Millander, which Sara confirms. After Gil poo-poo's any danger associated with his birthday, Catherine outlines everyone's errands: Nicky is analyzing the tape; Warrick and Sara are sent off to inspect the perimeter of the warehouse to determine how Millander got in and out. Catherine and Gil will examine the body.

Despite the rain, Warrick manages to find some prints, and notes that he must have taken off his boots before he stepped inside. The depth of Millander's footprints indicate that he carried the body inside.

Meanwhile, Catherine photographs the body in the tub. Gil looks up and notes that there is gunpowder sticking to tiny abrasions on the victim's cheek. Gil is puzzled. "From what I can tell, he was shot once in the chest. Unburned gunpowder wouldn't plume this way." Catherine turns her attention back to the tub and finds a long strand of brunette hair.

We hear the suicide message again, and the A/V tech says, "This wasn't recorded in a warehouse. There's no auditory echo." In fact, it may have been made in a car, with the man holding the tape recorder an inch from his mouth. A whirring noise is audible in the background but neither know what it is. There's something else on the recording-- a country-western song: Willie Hank's "Don't Pay the Ransom". He plans to call the local C&W stations to see when they played that song as it will help establish a timeline. The tech then points out that there is an imbalance in background sound during the recording The left speaker is blown out and somehow, they extrapolate from this that Paul Millander happened to be driving while the recording was made.

Meanwhile, Sara and Warrick are at the scene of Walker's retrieved car. The Nevada State Patrol found it. Warrick then wonders aloud, "How would Millander know that the guy who'd pick him up had a birthday August 17, 1957?" Sara and Brass do not have the answer to this question.

And at the morgue, the coroner x-rays Walker and confirms that the victim only suffered one gunshot wound. Gil wonders if the stippling (fragmented gunpowder on his face) might have arisen if Walker turned his face away from the gun; Al dismisses this as unlikely.

Across town, at the car, Warrick has found some gunshot residue on the ceiling above the passenger seat. Warrick lifts some of the residue from the ceiling fabric and a second bullet went out the window. We flash to Walker reading into the tape recorder while Millander points a gun at him, then Millander grazing Walker's face as he shoots, the bullet going out through the window. "I'm going to call Nick, tell him we found out what that unidentified whir sound was -- the bullet going out."

The hair Catherine found in the tub has a skin tag, which means it can be tested for DNA. Gil notes that the tag for the hair is aged, which may indicate that the murderer froze the hair and then placed it in the tub to confound investigators. Or, since the hair belongs to a woman, maybe it indicates that the next victim will be a female. However, neither he nor Catherine can say anything that will portend means or motive.

Meanwhile, Walker's car has been taken to CSI and Nicky has found a receptacle for all kinds of receipts and tiny papers. Greg, fascinated by the case, has made his way over to the car to look at it along with Nicky. As both men sit in the car, Nicky sees a number imprinted on the plastic lining of the drink caddy. He thinks that whatever the number came from, it happened in the summer, as the heat would cause ink to burn plastic.

At a meeting, the CSI's discuss the case and go through the evidence they have gathered. Nicky found out that "Don't Pay the Ransom" played from 1:47 to 1:51 AM. Frustrated, Gil tells his team that "None of it matters. This is one of the few cases where physical evidence isn't helping us much. I mean, look at context: the victim's birthday is always on the anniversary of the murder of Millander's father. Staged, like his father's death. A planted hair, a planted fingerprint, it's all biographical. He's using the evidence to tell us a story." AS soon as these words are out of his mouth, Brass comes in to announce that Walker had a job driving newly-released film reels between Valencia and Las Vegas, taking a regular route. Other than a speeding ticket issued in July, his record was clean. Thinking of the serial number in the cup holder, Nick brightens.

Nick then tells Brass the numbers found in the drink caddy and it turns up the victim's driving record. Gil asks Brass to run the names of the other two victims for traffic records. Royce Harmon had a horrific driving record; Stuart Rampler had tickets. All three were ticked to the same cop, Kevin Yarnell. We get to meet Kevin Yarnell as he joins the CSI team in the offices to be questioned. After Gil asks how many speeding tickets Yarnell issues a day, the cop gives them a lot of attitude and says with a snarky tone that he's a good cop, even going to court on his day off to sit in on cases where people have contested their tickets. He eventually gets around to telling them that there are three judges that sit in on traffic court and maybe they should be talking to them.

 Catherine decides this isn't too bad an idea. We see the bailiff commanding everyone to rise for the honorable Judge Mason who just so happens to be Paul Millander. The bailiff continues. Judge Mason's court is in the city of Mulberry in Nevada. As he sits down, Gil gets visibly agitated and after a moment of stunned silence, rushes the bailiff and tells him to arrest Judge Mason on suspicion of murder. The judge has Gil thrown in the slammer for contempt of court.

In the next scene, Gil is sitting in the cell when Millander appears and asks quietly, "Where are you from?" Gil tells him he knows exactly where he is from and who he is. Mason/Millander responds that he knows he looks like a man named Paul Millander because cops have visited him twice in the past year, and he saw Millander's pic in the paper. He then goes on to argue that there is a viable academic paper that proves the existence of a doppelganger, and that he must be Millander's. Gil offers to do a DNA test to clear everything right up. The judge declines, but asks Gil to dinner. When Catherine arrives to bail him out, he has her lift the prints that the judge left on the bars of the cell, and tells Catherine that he just might take the man up in his dinner invite.

Back at the lab, Sara asks Greg what happened with that hair found in the bathtub. It turns out that he has—but the weird thing is that it has endogenous testosterone in it. This is an anabolic steroid, not a naturally occurring chemical for women. Both are boondoggled.

In the next scene, the CSI team parks in front of a beautiful, big Tudor house and after looking closely at rain boots left by the door, rings the doorbell. Mrs. Mason opens the door, and after complimenting her on the home, asks long they've lived there. She says, "We bought the year we adopted Craig, so that would be '92." Mrs. Mason then goes off to prod Craig into saying hello. Craig then asks Gil if he'd like an ID tag "for safety." A little weird, but ok.

Over dinner, Mrs. Mason asks her husband to tell Gil where he picked up the boots Gil was admiring. She explains that her husband enjoys going bargain hunting, rain or shine, and the boots come in handy. As Mason is explaining how, as a traffic court judge, he takes safety seriously, little Craig snaps a Polaroid of Gil, startling the poor man thoroughly. "You'll be safe now," he assures him.

It's not long after that when Gil receives a call from Catherine telling him that the prints left on the bars of the cell match Judge Mason's prints, not the prints on file for Paul Milander. After Gil gets off the call, Mason explains that Gil has confused Mason with "a very bad man" so he "left him fingerprints". This pisses off Grissom and dinner is pretty much over.

Back at CSI, Gil faces yet another challenge in proving that Millander and Mason are the same person: the records building for Mulberry burned down in 1982, thus making the retracing of the judge's identity extremely challenging since he has no birth certificate. Fortunately, Brass has gone to the new records building and dug up records of current property tax payments for Paul and Isabelle Millander. Gil and Catherine drive over to the Millander neighborhood. A middle-aged woman opens the door, and Gil and Catherine, surprised, explain" We're with the Las Vegas Crime Lab --" Isabelle cuts her off and says, "Are you here about my husband? That happened over thirty years ago." Catherine responds with: "It's our understanding that your child witnessed your husband's murder." Isabelle lets them in and says, "My child was only ten..." and then trails off. As she catches Catherine looking at the dining room table, she says: "I always set a place for Paul.", as in her husband. Isabelle fills in that her husband Paul made hand molds and masks. We flash back to the scene last year where he held the latex hand with the fingerprints from the Roy Harmon murder. He quickly realizes that Millander had been using his father's molds -- and ergo, his father's fingerprints -- to plant at the crime scene.

Catherine excuses herself to go the restroom, and she leaves. She snoops as she makes her way there, opening doors until she stumbles across a little girl's room. A plaque identifies it as Pauline's room.

In the main room, Gil is looking over an old ashtray made from Paul Millander Sr.'s handprint, and Isabelle if he can take the ashtray to the lab for testing.

In the pink frilly girl's room, Catherine is looking at photos of a tomboyish little girl. She's going through drawers and notices a stack of baseball cards, and then walks over to the closet and opens the door. Just then Isabelle comes in and asks, "What are you doing in my daughter's room?" Catherine explains that she has a daughter and was admiring the room and the clothes. Isabelle looks upset and says her daughter died a long time ago. Gil asks, "What about your son?" They are hustled out of the house.

At the lab, Greg identifying the green substance on the ashtray as an alginate once used to make molds and special effects. Gil says, "These are his father's prints. He was planting them as his own." Catherine, meanwhile, is analyzing fingerprints she took from that stack of baseball cards she took from Pauline's room. Catherine says that she found no records of Pauline Millander's birth certificate, or even that she existed, but she did test the baseball card fingerprint against the prints of Paul Millander Jr, and they've got a match. This, then, means that Judge Mason is Paul Millander.

As soon as she is finished recounting this to Gil, they are summoned to the lab by Greg. He says that the hair from Pauline's room is female. And it matches the hair found in the tub at the crime scene. DNA identical. Catherine is tempted to conclude that Pauline planted it but Sara lets her in on a little phenomenon known as trans-genderism. She explains: "He planted it. He planted his own hair...Pauline was taking male hormone injections." Gil is just floored by this and gasps: why?? Sara says that Pauline had a sex change. There was no evidence of Paul as a child in the Millander house. Isabelle refused to talk about her daughter.

So, of course, the next scene is of Gil asking Isabelle: "Is this what you've been hiding? That your daughter is now your son?" Isabelle tells them that her daughter went away and came back a very strange man, and that she wouldn't let him in the house like that. Gil then asks for permission to collect hair from Pauline's bedroom.

Cut to Millander/Mason, in the interrogation tank. He says, "They told my parents I had an 'endocrinic ambiguity.' My chromosomes said female but my body wasn't that sure. The doctors told my parents to raise me as they saw fit." Gil and Millander now digress into a little story about how Millander was raised as both a girl and a boy, and "a boy could have saved his father." Gil swabs Millander for DNA evidence and Millander says he's already picked his next victim. Gil replies, "It doesn't matter. You'll be in jail."

We next learn that Millander's arraignment has been bumped from 8 AM to last on the schedule because he's acting as his own lawyer. Gil, his magical sixth sense powers piqued, runs down to Millander's holding room and finds only a neatly folded jumpsuit and a severed ID bracelet. We then see Millander in a suit, with a Las Vegas Police Department ID, walking through the detectors and out the door, waving at the security camera. Gil watches the tape. He remembers that the ID on top of his jacket when he was in contempt of court was photocopied. That and the Polaroid of him would make a sound enough ID to pass cursory inspection.

Much later, at CSI central, Catherine tells Gil that she thinks Millander slipped : they all have the "I love you, Mom" part of the suicide note, but Pete Walker had no mother. Gil says that he never slips, and sprints out the door, and then to his car to the Millander home. When he opens the unlocked door, he sees Isabelle at the table set for two. She's been stabbed. Gil heads to the bathroom, following the sound of a tape spool flopping over. As he opens the door, he sees Paul in the tuba tape perched at the rim: "My name is Paul Millander. I reside at 13891 Sand Creek Road. I'm 46 years of age, and I'm going to kill myself. I'd like to say 'I love you' to my mother, Isabelle. I'm so sorry. I never meant to put you through this. I just can't do it anymore. I've lost hope." Gil listens to the gunshot on the tape, then closes his eyes.

The Finger

It's daytime in Vegas, and an uneasy-looking middle-aged man walks into a bank with a large briefcase. He presents the teller a withdrawal slip filled out to the tune of $1 million, and says, "I'll need to make a withdrawal." But of course, one can't withdraw $1million in cash even if the cash in question is one's own. So managers and official people get involved and a reams of paperwork are filled out. At ten minutes 'til 5 pm we are given a view of the security tape: grainy black-and-white footage of the man waiting. We see a time-stamp for 5:36 PM, and the man get irritated as he waits. He finally has the money, and turns down an invitation to be escorted to his car. As he pulls out, he notices a police car driving slowly down the street and begins to drive until pulled over. The man looks stressed out. Very stressed out. His cell phone rings and the cop smirks and says, "You gonna get that?" and then notices that the man's knuckles are coated in blood. He is then asked to step out of the car.

We then find out via Catherine and Gil's conversation as they walk towards the interrogation tank that the man's name is Roy Logan. He is in real estate and sits on the mayor's committee to revitalize the downtown. As soon as he sees Catherine and Gil, he advises them that he's not saying anything without a lawyer. Catherine swabs the dried blood and asks him to strip. In the next scene, he's standing in his underwear while she takes photos of him. Not long after they tell him to get his clothes back on, his lawyer barges in and barks "What the hell is going on? Put your clothes back on, don't say another word to these people. I'm taking my complaint to the district attorney -- you had no grounds to detain Mr. Logan, let alone disrobe him." Gil informs the lawyer that his hands were covered in blood and he had a million dollars in his briefcase, and then Paul reminds him that it's not a crime to be rich. Paul and Logan hastily retreat, and though Logan is careful to pick up his cell phone, he appears to not see the sunglasses sitting next to them.

Catherine then asks Gil to drop off the swabs at the lab; she's got to go to Lindsey's school recital. She starts to leave, notices the abandoned sunglasses, and grabs them on her way out. Logan is still in the parking lot. She walks over and gives him the sunglasses, and Logan, looking scared, says "You don't understand. Get away from me." The cell rings, and Logan answers it. He hands it over to Catherine, saying, "It's for you." Naturally, Catherine is puzzled but gets on the phone and identifies herself as "CSI 3 Willows". The voice of the end of the line establishes that she's not a cop, but she is a criminalist, and bully for all concerned cause if she had been a cop "she'd already be dead." Catherine asks who would be dead, but then the voice commands her to put her weapon on the ground, along with her pager, cell phone, and that case she is holding. She is warned that if she goes back into the police station, Amanda will be dead. She will also be dead if Catherine contacts any coworkers. She is then instructed to get back in the car and drive anywhere but here, and await the next call.

Catherine glances around the darkened parking lot while she slowly lays her things on the ground. Then Catherine and Logan get in the car. As she is driving off, Gil happens to leave the building and notices Catherine behind the wheel, looking pretty pissed off. He whips out his cell and dials her number and then hears the phone ring a few feet away.

At the lab, Brass comes in just as we learn that the blood on Logan's knuckles is from a female. Brass exposits that Logan's a married family man with no record, and his vehicle has now been labeled with a Code 5, meaning "keep under surveillance, but do not make contact with the occupants." Brass sees how concerned Gil looks and reminds him that Catherine has a gun. He does not seemed comforted and walks off.

Catherine and Logan and Catherine asks: "who's Amanda?" Logan admits that Amanda is his girlfriend and we can see the steam coming from Catherine's ears. Apparently his wife doesn't know. Catherine asks how the voice on the phone made contact in the first place. Logan says that he left many messages for Amanda, and didn't hear from her, he went over to her condo. On the bed, he found an altoid tin with a severed human finger inside. The moment he picked it up and saw what it was, his cell phone rang. The caller wanted million dollars in cash by the end of the day, or he would send the rest of her. Catherine sighs and informs him that she needs a drink.

At around that time, Sara is on a date with the guy who gave her the duffel bag filled with the gooey remains of a Viet Nam war vet a few episodes back. As they make small talk, she notices Catherine and Logan parking across the street, and watches the two of them walk by. Catherine sees Sara too, and keeps on going. Sara's date asks if that isn't Catherine, one of her co-workers. Sara, looking somewhat unhappy to see Catherine, replies that it is. The camera swoops over to Catherine and Logan sitting at the diner counter and Catherine commands Logan to order something, since it's not like they're on a set schedule. Logan is initially outraged, wanting to be sitting in the car waiting for the phone to ring. Catherine informs him that a cell phone is also called a mobile phone because it is mobile. And it will ring in the diner just as loudly. Catherine orders two glasses, one with ice, one without. Roy Logan orders coffee.

At CSI, Warrick thinks Logan may have wanted to confess and bring Catherine to the body. Nicky says that if that were true, Catherine wouldn't have left her stuff behind. Brass has checked out Mrs. Logan and she isn't the victim. They resign themselves to the fact that they have to wait until an actual crime has been committed.

At the diner, Catherine is using the ice to preserve the finger. The phone rings and tells Catherine to drive to the Horseshoe Tavern. She has an hour to get there. On her way out, she puts the glass down on Sara's table. The date wants to know if it is a finger. Sara picks up the glass to confirm that it is, indeed, a finger, and as she follows Catherine to the street, Catherine gets back in the car and drives away.

In the car, Catherine orders Logan to mark the edges of the money with the makeup wand she would have used for Lindsay at her recital. It glows in the dark since Lindsay was playing the Moon. She laments that she missed her daughter's recital. A cop passes and Logan momentarily freaks out. The cop, however, does nothing.

Back at CSI Central, Sara explains that she made no eye contact--just dropped the finger and walked out. Gil confirms that it was the right index finger. Gil sighs and enumerates the oddities that have been thrown at him: "A severed finger, a million bucks, and Catherine's not allowed to talk to anyone?" They prepare to scatter so they can begin talking to Mrs. Logan. Sara comments that it was a big coincidence that Catherine showed up at the same place she was, but then some of her colleagues admit that they were nosy, and had found out where her date was going to be and with whom.

They pass the Horseshoe Tavern so Catherine makes a U-turn at lightning speed and flies into the parking lot, making deep tire tracks. She then walks with Logan toward the tavern and headlights shine in their face. Silhouetted against the lights is a man in a rabbit suit. He demands the briefcase and as Logan goes to hand it over, Catherine stops him and demands, "First we need to see Amanda." The Rabbit refuses. Hex tells them that they need to get back in the car, drive to a gas station in Henderson, and wait by pay phone there to await further instructions. Catherine says no, and the Rabbit shrugs and says that Amanda will die, and walks back to the car. Logan runs up and gives Harvey the briefcase.
Several hours later during daylight, Brass and Nicky go out to pay Mrs. Logan a visit. She is a typical housebound

trophy wife, looking as though she spends her days at the mall, the gym, and the spa. They do not learn much: Mrs. Logan's keeping quiet as lawyer Paul's had advised her.

At around this time, Katherine and Logan pull up at an abandoned service station and look for a pay phone. They find it, but it's mangled and broken. Logan immediately freaks out but Catherine reminds him that "He had a shotgun. If all he wanted was the money, we'd both be dead." Catherine looks at the phone booth and notices that stuffed in the pages of the hanging phone book is a new map with an X on it. She then tells Logan to give her the phone and again, he has a fit.

At CSI, Greg, Gil, and Nicky hypothesize that Mrs. Logan did not see the severed finger, and that it clearly didn't belong to her. Gil and Nicky announce their a warrant to go to Logan's townhouse. As Nicky leaves, Warrick tells Gil that Logan is leaving the gas station according to the state trooper who spotted the car earlier. Gil heads out.

Gil, Sara, and Warrick get out at the Horseshoe Tavern, and immediately notice the evidence Catherine left for them. Warrick takes photos of the footprints, and Gil finds a helium canister. They think it was used to disguise a voice. At the townhouse, Nikcy breaks in and is greeted by a cockatiel squawks in response. He plays the answering machine. There are many messages to Amanda from Logan. There are two half-filled wineglasses on the counter with lipstick on them. Nicky inspects the bird; its feathers are stained in the front.

Meanwhile, Catherine and Logan are at a place that looks to process sewage or reclaimed water or something. Catherine notices a grill covering a drain. Amanda is in the drain, but she is floating facedown in the water.

At the morgue, the coroner Gil that the finger was severed postmortem with a serrated blade. After he finishes, Gil's cell rings. It's Catherine. Gil beats her to the punch and says: "She's dead. And whoever touched the money probably has glow-in-the-dark paint on their hands."

After commercial break, we see Catherine's walking down the hall with Warrick. Lindsay had come to the lab after her recital. She helped Greg in the lab and then fell asleep. They stop in the break room, where Lindsey is asleep, still in her glow in the dark paint. Catherine tiptoes in and sits on the edge of the couch where Lindsey's sleeping, and then reaches out to touch her daughter's hair when Catherine's cell phone rings.

She then goes to the morgue to find out what the story is on Amanda's body. The coroner says she's been in the water about twenty-four hours. He directs Catherine and Gil's attention to the head of the body and pulls out Amanda's tongue; beneath it is a thriving colony of blowfly eggs. David notes that they're waterlogged. This means were there before Amanda was dunked. She has been dead for at least 48 hours. Catherine notices the bloody nose and bruising; Amanda died from blunt-force trauma. She has a huge head wound with a shard of granite in it.

Catherine steps out and promptly runs into Logan, who demands to see the body. As soon as he does, he goes into hysterics. If only he'd paid sooner, if only, if only, he says. Gil says, "It wouldn't have made any difference. She was dead long before you could have helped her." Logan asks when they'll have an estimated time of death for Amanda. Catherine sends him out and Logan tells her that he can't face his wife.

She then goes to the town house where Nick is spraying luminol and uncovers a large patch of blood. He kneels next to the marble coffee table and notices a chip missing. Catherine thinks the kidnappers broke in and beat Amanda up. Indeed, there is blood everywhere. Even on the bird. The fact that there is not a trail of blood out the door indicates that Amanda was wrapped in something. The serrated knife used to cut off her finger is in the dishwasher, freshly washed. Catherine sends the wineglasses to the lab. She moves over to the fridge and notices a picture of Amanda in the shower, smiling from behind a patterned shower curtain liner. She goes to the bathroom and finds a terrycloth curtain, but no plastic patterned liner. It has been ripped out. It is later discovered by Warrick and Sara in the drain where Amanda was found dead.

Brass and Gil, meanwhile, go through Amanda's phone records. The same four numbers were called a lot: her mom, a pizza place, Logan, and the gym, but Amanda's last logged call is to Mrs. Logan's cell. The wine glasses, when back from the lab, reveal two sets of female DNA. One Amanda's, one unknown.

Meanwhile, Sara and Warrick are working on the shower curtain together, and Sara finds a small cut in the curtain and a peanut butter stain. Nicky flashes back to when they went to interview Mrs Logan, and remembers that her child was eating a peanut butter sandwich in the back seat of the car. They immediately apprehend the Logan SUV and find a patch of carpet with a dark blotch. Peanut butter.

The next scene is of Catherine, Mrs. Logan, and Paul the lawyer in the interrogation tank. Catherine asks if Mrs. Logan knew Amanda, because Amanda called on the last morning of her life, and they talked for about for three minutes and fifty-five seconds. Gil ignores the lawyer and tells the group his theory: Mrs. Logan went over to Amanda's place to confront her about sleeping with her husband, and a drink turned into a Jerry Springer style brawl. Mrs. Logan wrapped the body in a shower curtain, sliced off a finger, and moved the body. Mrs. Logan then chooses to break her silence and says: "I listened to her rantings about how she and Roy were going to get married, and I set her straight. Roy was not going to leave me for her. He loved his money more than he loved the both of us. I told her I was going to evict her from that tacky little townhouse, and then Roy came in. You should have seen the look on his face. And I left them there to work it out." Catherine listens politely and then asks Brass to hit the lights. Mrs. Logan's hands aren't glowing, but Paul's are.

Paul admits that he put on a mask, and made a phone call, but that technically he didn't break the law. He says he merely did what his client asked him to do, and didn't know anything about anyone being dead. Logan set the entire thing up as a way to cover up a murder and get out of Vegas with a million bucks in cash. He says he knows that Logan withdrew lots of cash and stowed a million dollars in a country club locker room, but figured he was just hiding assets from his wife. Gil goes to check out the locker and Catherine and Brass stop by Logan's hotel room. He's gone. At the club, the locker is empty.

They huddle to put the pieces together: the mistress called the wife and told her about their relationship. The wife came over. Logan came over and saw them together. The wife left. Logan kills Amanda, cleans up the crime scene, calls his lawyer, and asks him to help. Everything, including picking Catherine up, was planned out in advance. Nicky asks why Logan drew a map to take Catherine to the body; Gil says that without a body, Logan would be under suspicion. The CSIs quickly come to the conclusion that he wanted to set up his wife for the blame, and the money-marking further took suspicion away from him.

Just then, Catherine's cell phone rings. Logan has been picked up for reckless driving, and is being detained. Catherine stops by Logan's cell to visit him. She says coolly: "You're short one mistress. I got to hand it to you, that was a brilliant performance. But then again, any man who juggles a wife and a mistress and God knows what else has to be a pro." Logan shrugs and says he was so used to lying why not lie more? Catherine says, "Try explaining that to your son." Then she leaves.

Burden of Proof

It is night, somewhere in the countryside outside of Vegas. Gil's flashlight beam falls on the body of a nude women, laying bruised and insect-ridden on the ground. Near the body is an old truck that appears to have broken down. Behind the wheel is a dead man with a rat on him.

There is also a third body, and as Gil looks at it, another man says: "That one's not ours. I authorize all cadavers and associated research. He's not ours." As it turns out, he and man are in an enclosed area with a sign that helpfully reads: "Anthropology Department. Private Property. Keep Out." Brass and Catherine walk in and seems sort of appalled that people donate their body to science and end up submerged in a pond or crammed in a car. Catherine pronounces the place a "body farm" and says it's creepy. Gil disagrees and offers a gentler label: a controlled study of situational decomposition. All in all, a very healthy place. Brass then says:: "Whoever dumped the body here knew about the body farm. What he didn't know is that each body is tracked by a bunch of scientists." There is no rigor mortis, so the body was dumped less than six hours ago.

The CSIs examine the body. There is a gunshot wound to the chest. A beetle climbs out from under the victim's shirt: a carpet beetle. These creatures, Gil explains, are the last to arrive at a corpse, when it's almost a skeleton. Ah—there is a skeleton hanging on a tree covered in carpet beetles. He immediately directs that the body is removed since it is falling victim to cross contamination.

At CSI, the staff is dismayed to find that Gil is putting strange experiments in the community fridge in the kitchen. He is testing horizontal bloodstains vis-à-vis surface textures and does anyone have linoleum at home he could use? Nick complains that the blood in the fridge smells awful but Gil takes this as a request for knowledge as to where the blood came from, "That's why the Red Cross gives it to us, because it's past its expiration date." He then takes off for the coroner.

The body from the body farm is on the table. The wound in the front of the body's torso would indicate being hit by a projectile, but there is no bullet hole and no exit wound. They decide to slice out the wound area and do a more thorough search. Catherine comes into announce that she's ID'd the body: it's Mike Kimble. He is 38, and has a townhouse in Summerlin which Catherine decides to check up on while Gil stays behind to explore the wound area.

Catherine and Warrick arrives at the town house along with the fire department. The condo has been gutted by fire. There's s a flare-up, and a small explosion. While this is going on, Brass is interviewing the next-door neighbor, and learns the Kimble had a fiancée named Jane Bradley

Meanwhile, there's no bullet in the wound tract but there is a threaded screw, and a maggot that is found in cows. Gil notes that the body farm studies animals other than humans and has to figure out if this evidences cross contamination or something else.

After the fire dies down, Warrick and Nicky enter the house. They note immediately that it was arson, and head upstairs to the bedroom. Upon seeing a bloodstain on the floor, they conclude that it was a cover up.

Catherine and Brass pay a visit to the fiancée. A teenage girl answers the door without bothering to get off the phone and she continues her conversation as she lets Catherine and Brass in the house. They break the news to Jane. She takes it pretty well, considering. "This can't be happening. Mike is dead? I don't know how I'm going to tell my kids. They love Mike." Jane says that she was to have married Mike in a week at the Tangiers (which is a fictional casino btw, also used in the movie Casino). After pausing to reprimand her son about eating candy after ten pm, she tells Catherine and Warrick that Mike was a photographer. Just then, the ex-husband, Russ Bradley, shows up to argue with her about the fact that the kids aren't ready to go to his house yet, and her end of the deal with joint custody etc. The argument ends abruptly when Bradley finds out that Mike's dead. Jane's reaction -- a small smile and a reluctance to look him in the eye -- is kinda weird. Catherine asks to see Bradley's hands, and he says: " I stop paying alimony the day Mike and Jane get married. I'm the last guy who would have killed him." He gives Catherine his business card and goes into the den to pick up the kids.

Back at the Kimble condo, Gil stops by when Nicky is in the middle of determining what accelerant was used. Gil then goes to the home office, which, oddly, was barely touched by the fire. Gil hones in on a framed shot of Jane, Mike, and Jane's two kids; Jane and the kids holding a poster board with the words, "Mike, welcome to the family." Wedged behind this photo is another one. Gil pulls apart the picture frame so we can see a handful of pictures of Jane's daughter, each one in a progressively more, shall we say, inappropriate position. Gil doesn't say anything. Nicky gets visibly upset.

Catherine and Brass are given the delightful task of telling Jane that Kimble may have had relations with her daughter, Jody. Jane is in denial. Catherine sits Jody down and tells her that the CSIs found pictures in Kimble's house. Jane says urgently, "Tell her Mike would never do anything to hurt you." And then turns to Catherine and says "He truly was a father to both of the kids." Catherine tries to walk Jody through the pictures but Jody denies the whole thing. Catherine says firmly, "Anything he did to you was not your fault." Jody only answers with, "I loved Mike, and he loved me." Jane looks disturbed by this. Catherine leaves and through the window, watches Jane silently sit on the arm of Jody's chair, leaning against her.

Warrick is assigned the disturbing task of blowing up one of Jody's pictures for analysis, and it turns out that the photo was taken by a camera that matches one that Kimble was known to use. Warrick explains that he's trying to clear up the picture. Nicky notices a smudge at the bottom right-hand corner of the photo—it appears to be the finger of the photographer.

Meanwhile, Gil is inspecting fly-covered rotting beef in an effort to figure out how cow maggots and cow tissue got into the body. Sara stops by, hurt that she isn't involved in the experiment. When he takes off, and asks her to clean it up, she gets even more angry that he doesn't realize she's a vegetarian. Gil, unaware of the real issue, tells her to tell

Greg to do it, and continues on his way, off to inspect one of Bradley's firearms.

Brass, meanwhile, is talking to Bradley about his daughter. Bradley, angered, tells Brass that Kimble was too touchy-feely. They are soon joined by Gil, who has arrived to inspect Bradley's firearm. He notes that it's been cleaned and Bradley replies, "Of course. You never store a dirty firearm." Gil asks what kind of ammunition Bradley uses and Brass answers for him, "A .38 special. It takes .38s." Gil is visibly annoyed.

Back in the lab, as Sara fills out paperwork, Warrick stops by and tells her that the accelerant was nail polish. He reminds her of her stat that 94% of arsonists are male, and tells her that this must have been one of the other 6%. He leaves and she appears pensive.

Cut to Jody, getting examined at the hospital when Catherine notices a burn mark on her arm. Jody says it's from a curling iron but Catherine clearly looks skeptical. She exits when Jody gets her rape kit done. As it turns out, when the doctor finished the exam on Jody, he found evidence of chronic sexual abuse. Catherine tells this to Gil as he's molding ground beef into little balls and putting them in the freezer to test his new theory that the man was shot with a frozen beef pellet.

Catherine and Nicky then search Jane's home until they find a dirty nightgown of Jody's, shoved into the dirty clothes hamper and covered with semen stains. Catherine tells Jane, "Child services will be remanding Jody to a foster home." Jane, still not getting it, or not wanting to, asks if her fiancée was " Brass teleports into the scene to tell us all that Kimble was not, in fact, Jane's fiancée because Jane cancelled the wedding five days ago. She stands by her assertion, however, that Kimble wouldn't have done whatever he was accused of.

The DNA, as it turns out, is not Kimble's. Greg reveals whose semen is on Jody's nightshirt: her brother Jake's. The next scene is of a hysterical young man stammering that he never did anything like that to his sister but can't explain how his semen got on her nightgown. Brass tells Bradley and Jane that the county will be providing Jake with an advocate, and the rest of the questioning will proceed from there.

When the advocate arrives, Brass asks if Jake took pictures of his sister and planted them in Kimble's house. His advocate answers for him that he didn't and has no idea how his DNA was on his sister's nightgown. Brass snaps back, "Maybe a little hobbit put it there." This sends Jake even closer to the verge of tears, and before the advocate grabs Jake and runs, Nicky convinces everyone to let him

talk to Jake alone. Once alone, he calmly tells the boy that
everyone does it, even while sleeping. Jake nods silently
and Nicky says, "And then you go to take a leak, dust off
the equipment, you just grab the first thing that's handy,
hmmm?" Jake sighs and says that his sister's nightgown
just happened to be on the edge of the hamper. They both
sort of giggle over the whole thing, and Nicky then tells
Jake, "Even if the situation's embarrassing, honesty is
probably the best policy." They laugh and bond. Nicky then
asks if Kimble acted odd around Jody. According to Jake,
Jody was the one acting weird, always looking forward to
Mike's visits a little to eagerly.

After shooting his frozen meat bullets and analyzing the
outcome, Gil and Brass meet with Bradley and begin
outlining their case. They tell him that they found meat in
his gun loader. Bradley gets angry and says that Kimble
was touching his daughter and made a really rude
comment along the lines of "like mother like daughter" and
it got out of hand. Brass then tells us the details: Bradley's
grocery store chain drops off carcasses at the body farm, so
he knew where it was. After dropping off the body, he
returned to the house to burn up the evidence.

Gil is then ready to turn his attention to the child
molestation issue when Sara appears in his doorway with a
request for a six month leave of absence because she

doesn't feel like he respects her. He asks if it's about the meat thing and she gets pissed. She says that this is not some quirk and the problem is not just about her. She gets even more annoyed and says that if he doesn't grant her the leave, she'll quit. As she's exiting, Gil says, "The lab needs you here."

After the commercial break, he finds Catherine at the lab and tells her Bradley copped a plea to the murder and the DA expedited it. Catherine, who appears to have worn one of her daughter's tank tops to work, says that it's his first offense and it's voluntary manslaughter so he'll be free in four years. No jury is going to convict a father for killing his daughter's abuser. Gil shows Catherine Jody's nail polish remover, which happens to match the accelerant used in the fire. But Catherine's lab work has concluded that Jody really did burn herself on a curling iron.

Meanwhile, Warrick is still working on that photo, zooming in on Jody's eye to amplify the reflection in them. It looks like the picture was taken on a boat. Kimble did not own a boat but Bradley did. Warrick goes to it and snaps photos of the boat's porthole for comparison.

Catherine then tells Jody that she knows Mike gave her his camera and then her father used it to take pictures of her on his boat, then possibly placing the camera back at

Mike's place to implicate him, along with the pictures..
Jody says quietly, "He said I was like my mom, when she
was young and they were happy. He said having me was
like having his family back." She says she tried indirectly to
tell her mom but it never came out clear enough. So she
told Mike, and he said he was going to fix things, so her
dad killed him. Warrick then appears and pulls Catherine
aside. The next scene is of Gil, Brass, Bradley, and his
lawyer. Gil says they found something on the boat: a
sleeping bag stained with vaginal and seminal fluid,
matching Jody and Bradley respectively. Bradley pleas with
his lawyer to make him a deal but he can't—Jody is twelve,
and in Nevada, the sexual assault of a minor aged fourteen
and under is a mandatory life sentence with no possibility
of parole. Bradley doesn't take this well.

Later, Gil and Catherine have dinner at Gil's, and she says
she heard about Sara. Grissom says yes, Sara is emotional.
Catherine laughs at this, and possibly feeling a little loose
from the wine, tells him: "You have to deal with it! You
have to deal with it! You have to deal with it first before
it...goes away. You are the supervisor. You have
responsibilities and people are making a family around you
whether you like it or not, whether you give them
permission or not." He eventually agrees and she then sits
on the couch while Gil gets on the phone. He says: "Yeah.
Hi. I-I'd like to get some flowers for a girl. Oh, no. Not

flowers. Um, uh, uh, a plant. A living plant. She likes vegetation. Yeah, that'd be fine. To a Sara Sidle, delivered at the CSI division of the Las Vegas Police Department, the one out on North Trop boulevard. Yeah, you can bill me at the same place. Gil Grissom. The sentiment? Oh, oh, on the card. Ummm. Uhhh. Have, have it say...uh, have it say, uh, 'From Grissom.' Thank you."

Primum Non Nocere

At a weekend league hockey game, a man is checked into the side of the rink and gets a nosebleed and a laceration on his face. The doctor examines him, gives him a stitch or two, and sends him back on the ice, and play resumes. After an intense montage of stick work and flying chips of ice, a fight breaks up. When it's broken up, the stitched player is unconscious on the ice.

The next scene is of Gil and Catherine entering the rink. The body has been moved to the bench. He was able to get himself there with some assistance, and then died three minutes later. In addition to the minor laceration he sustained to his face, he has a large gash on his neck. In the bleachers, Gil peruses the list of the dead mans penalties: "Two minutes for elbowing. Four minutes for high sticking. Ten minutes for unsportsmanlike conduct." He and Sara then grudgingly and carefully make their way across the ice. They find wood splinters in it, and frozen blood. Cut to a montage of them walking over the ice. They find bleached-wood splinters embedded in the white ice. As they scrape up samples, they hear the whir of the zamboni come to erase the evidence left on the crime scene.

In the men's locker room, Catherine interviews the doctor. She establishes that the victim (named Terry Rivers) was breathing when carried off the ice, but died on the bench. CPR proved futile. Catherine asks about the stitches and the doctor stresses that he advised River to rest and stay out of the game, but Rivers chose not to take his advice. She asks what this weekend league plays for—money? A chance to beat people up? And a burly man named Tommy Sconzo, who is missing a few teeth, replies that it's for the pride.

Not ready to give up on the fact that the Zamboni disrupted the scene, Gil wheels a mirror under it, and finds a tooth embedded in a chunk of ice on the horizontal screw. Sara ponders the large mountain of ice shavings left behind the Zamboni and measures it. Gil estimates that it'll melt at about fifty cubic feet per hour.

Over at the B plot, Nicky and Warrick are walking through Ceasar's, eventually coming upon homicide detective Lockwood, who tells Nicky the DFO's in the back. The victim is Stan Grevey, 35, backup sax player -- who's lying slumped over a table. Nicky notices what he calls "tiny scrubbing bubbles" in the mouth of the deceased. Warrick points out that the tiny bubbles have been wiped down. There is also cowhide between Grevey's teeth; they look at his arm and note that he tied himself off. The evidence thus far points to an OD but there is no paraphernalia. Still, they gather some of the white powder on the table to take back to the lab, and a lone contact lens. They are interrupted when a lounge singer makes her way towards the stiff, asking how he's doing. She is dismayed to learn that he's not doing well. In fact, he's dead.

Back at CSI Central, the coroner tells Gil that Rivers's tox screen just showed quinine, indicating that he had malaria in the past six months, or he likes G and T's. He also has a hairline fracture of the ulna, bruised kidney, ten stitches off the orbital bone, fracture of the nasal bone, and recently healed rib fractures. When he wasn't busy getting pummeled on the ice, he was, apparently, a stock broker. The coroner remains a tadbit confounded as to exactly how he died: it could have been the cut across his carotid, or the significant trauma the basilar artery also suffered, or the blood flooding through the intimal space and possibly causing syncope. It's also unclear as to whether his fall caused his death, or the other way around.

Still at the hockey ring, Catherine and Brass have been collecting hockey equipment and talking to people about Rivers. They have learned he was not a favorite. Catherine heads outside to question the last person on the hockey team roster, one Jane Gallagher. Catherine catches Jane as she's heading toward her motorcycle. Jane is sort of a unpleasant as well. After giving Catherine attitude replete with tacit accusations of sexism on Catherine's part ("I just warmed the bench. I'm just a girl. I didn't see anything. I'm just a girl, etc.) Catherine handles it gracefully.

Back at Greg's lab, we learn about the B plot. It turns out that the white powder taken from the scene is Mannitol— baby laxative used with heroin. The sample also contained China White, 91% pure.

Meanwhile, Catherine and Gil are walking into Rivers's apartment—a modern, industrial looking loft. After judging his taste in décor and theorizing about his ability to connect with others, Catherine kneels down to scan the bed with an ultraviolet light and discovers that he has had many a female companion between those sheets.

And at CSI central, Greg tries to flirt with Sara while she examines the hockey equipment collected from the rink. looking at the array of blades Sara is currently spraying with luminol. Greg, who has some experience with ice hockey, notes that blades a quarter inch in width could slice someone's throat, but it would take a pretty agile skater to be able to play effectively on blades that narrow. As it turns out, there is a set of blades that narrow: Jane's.

At the B plot, which I am actually not that interested in for some reason, Warrick and Nick dig through the garbage outside the casino and find that the victim's missing drug paraphernalia are in a dumpster, wrapped in Lillie's scarf. (Lillie is the lounge singer that wanted to know how the victim was doing).

Lille admits that the scarf is hers, but anyone could have picked it up. Of course, as Warrick and Nick walked in the casino towards the crime scene, she was on stage, wearing that scarf. Nicky and Warrick didn't notice, I guess. They ask for her prints so they can compare them with prints found on the scarf and/or drug gear.

Sara and Brass, meanwhile, have learned a thing or two about Rivers. He had managed to lose his teammates thousands of dollars via a stock scheme. Shortly after this happened, Jane had switched from this team to the opposing team. Gil, Sara, and Brass confront her at the UNLV basketball court and tell her that her skate was the one that nicked Rivers's carotid artery. Jane tells them that there was a pileup, ten guys had blades on, and everything was a blur. The victim was a stationary target beneath ten people. Gil reminds her that she'd said she hadn't seen anything and Jane barfs on his shoes. Jane says weakly, "I knew I shouldn't have had that shrimp salad last night," and goes to flag down a janitor to get it cleaned up. Gil then stoops down and collects some of the vomit for evidence. Ewww. The vomit, as it turns out, is crustacean-free. She does, however, have morning sickness. There was blood in the sample, which is common in early pregnancy. They wonder if Rivers was the father, and a get a warrant to search Jane's apartment.

In the B-plot, the prints Nicky found match a musician in Lillie's backup band named Bill; and the prints were on Grevey's works. Bill explains that he cleaned up the scene because Grevey's got a son, and he didn't want the son to know that his father had died foaming at the mouth in a casino with a needle in his arm. We then find out that Bill met Grevey in AA; Warrick asks Bill as how Lillie's scarf got involved; Bill avoids Warricks eyes and tells him that the scarf just happened to be there. They ask him to roll up his sleeves. He does. There are no track marks so they decide he wasn't using.

Cut to Lillie walking down a hall toward the lounge, listening to piano music as she walks. As she enters the empty lounge, we see that Warrick is the one playing the tune that she is enjoying. Lillie stops to watch him, and he stops playing as soon as he notices her. After some chit chat, he asks Lillie how well she knows the band she plays with. Lillie answers, "Well enough."

Meanwhile, Gil and Sara are checking out Jane's sheets in the lab. There are semen stains everywhere. As Gil's unfolding the fitted sheet, toenail clippings fall out. Sara says softly, "With all the sex these people are having, maybe I should play hockey."

Back at the lounge, Lillie has learned that the composition Warrick is playing is his own, and she asks him why he doesn't try to make it in show biz, telling him that he is essentially a nobody since he spends most of his days in a lab examining, oh, shards of glass and vacuum cleaner bags. She bids him good day and takes off to go sing at the cocktail lounge. As he, too, gets up to go, he notices the bartender trying to covertly slip a packet of heroin between two coasters, and then put a drink on the coaster/heroin sandwich.

Back at the A plot, we learn that the tooth Sara and Gil found in the Zamboni matches the toenail found in Jane's bed. Or, "Whoever was in Jane Gallagher's bed was on the ice the night Terry Rivers died." The man to whom the toenails and tooth belong: Sconzo. He admits to seeing Jane, and says that he treated her far better than Rivers did. He seems bitter about this. He also seems bitter about the fact that Rivers' stock market scheme lost him $12,000. They remind him that he's the leader of his team, the rat pack, and Gil tells a little story about a bunch of Chinese guys who wanted someone dead, so they all bit him. That way, none of them could be charged with murder cause no one would know who delivered the lethal bite. Gil wonders if he got his team to take out Rivers in the same manner. Their little meeting comes to an end after Sconzo's beeper goes off.

At the morgue, the coroner tells Gil that Rivers had Wolff-Parkinson-White syndrome, a cardiac condition that can lead to extremely rapid heart rates. This can result in palpitations, light-headedness, or loss of consciousness. Quinine can also be lethal for someone with this condition.

And at the B plot, Warrick tells Nicky about the bartender's sleight of hand with the coasters. Nicky kind of knew that and says that Lillie uses as well, and gets her heroin from the same bartender.. Warrick doesn't seem particularly happy to hear that.

Later, Gil and Sara are talking to Jane, who tells them of the time she and Rivers were in bed together and he just went soft and passed out. She called the team doctor and the team doctor told her to get him rushed to the ER, which she did. Sara asks if she was dating Rivers and Sconzo at the same time and she says she was dating Rivers and sleeping with Sconzo. After this interview, Gil, Catherine, and Sara reconvene to go over what they know:

there was no quinine in Rivers's apartment, no indication from his medical records that he had had malaria, nor any indication that it was prescribed. Jane not only had access to quinine, she didn't know quinine could kill him. Catherine notes that someone with access to medical records could do so.

So of course, they hightail to talk to the doc. The doctor admits to giving Rivers quinine at the last game. Why? He was in love with Jane and thought that Rivers had fathered her child. Gil gleefully breaks the news to the doctor that he killed the wrong guy, and thus ends plot A.

Now to wrap up plot B: the bartender gets arrested for dealing and then Warrick decides to find Lillie and talk to her one-on-one. He then goes to the nearest table and gambles.

Felonious Monk

The episode begins at a Buddhist temple that is allegedly down the street from the Luxor. Inside the pristine interior, a monk sits still in meditation. He is interrupted when he hears the click of a trigger. He opens his eyes, and then we see blood splatter.

In the next shot, Nicky meets Sara and Gil near the entrance to the temple, telling them that the paramedics told him there are four dead with no witnesses. We see a monk in saffron robes standing a short distance a way. As it turned out, he's the one that flagged down the cops.

They enter the temple and Gil tells them to walk close to the walls lest they disturb evidence. They arrive at the room where the four monks were shot. Nothing seems to be missing, which leads them to conclude it was a hit, not a robbery. They were shot one at a time at close range.

Gil turns to exploring the Zen garden in the back, taking care not to sully the raked sand with his shoeprints. He notices a rifle, laid down in a cluster of wood. Meanwhile O'Reilly interviews one of the monks. He learns that they came from Thailand to share the treasures of Buddhism with Nevada. Most of the other monks are on a retreat, due back tomorrow. They are raising money to build a school, and he didn't see anything because he was at the bank making a deposit. He asks the monk if they've ever had problems in the past, and the monk quietly replies "The past is in the past."

In the Plot B, Catherine enters a cop bar and sees a friend that she identifies as Jimmy Tadero. They politely chit chat, and it turns out the Catherine learned a lot about criminology from this guy. He also seems to be on the verge of retirement. They discuss the Logan case and Jimmy says he wished that Logan had gotten the chair. On the bar TV, a news report comes on: Dwight Kelso in a hospital bed, admitting that he shot a man, he didn't kill Stephanie Watson. Catherine seems to think there could be a shred of truth to that but her companion disagrees. We see a flashback: a woman exiting a strip club and getting stabbed, and landing on the pavement near a puddle. Jimmy points out that witnesses saw Kelso harassing Stephanie in the strip club, and Kelso had a knife cut on his hand. Catherine, who it turns out knew Stephanie, says that maybe she just needs to accept that Stephanie is dead.

The next scene is of Catherine and Warrick in a cold-storage room, rooting through its contents to find the evidence kit from Stephanie's murder. They dig around and find the correct box. She flashbacks to her past life as a stripper and we learn that Stephanie was her colleague, and best friend. She pulls a G-string out of the box, and then a bloody knife.

Meanwhile, O'Reilly is interviewing David, the part time cook at the temple. He has no key to the place because the door is apparently always open. He says that he doesn't know of a history of violence or robbery, but gangs did tag the wall of the temple, and Ananda, the monk O'Reilly first interviewed, said he didn't wish to report it.

While David is being interviewed, Sara, Gil, and Nicky comb through the interior of the temple for evidence. Sara manages to find a boot print and a wad of gum smeared on a statue. Nicky finds a porn mag called "Big Bodacious Babes." This, for some reason, sends him into a fit of rage and indignation, deciding that a monk that hid porn probably shot other monks too, and protesting at the fact that he has to take his shoes off to be in the temple.

In the morgue, we learn that all the monks were shot in the third eye, a.k.a the sixth chakra, which is the vortex of consciousness. We are treated to a lesson on metaphysical anatomy, and learn that each chakra has a color and a vibration. Muladhara, the root chakra, keeps us in the grounded in the physical world. We also have Svadisthana, seat of sexual energy; Manipura, melting pot of spiritual and earthly desires; Anahata, the loving heart; Vishudda, where feelings are given expression; Ajna, the third eye; and finally Sahasrara, the crown connecting the mortal human to the timeless universe. The killer seemed to be familiar with the third eye; therefore, Gil decides, the killer is Buddhist. (They have chakra charts in every yoga studio in the western world. So it's possible that the killer is just into yoga. But whatever.)

Over at Plot B, Catherine has taken the bloody knife to Greg. He showes her where Eddie swabbed the blade fifteen years go, and that there are two people's blood on it: Stephanie Watson and Dwight Kelso's. The blood samples matched perfectly. Catherine sets the knife under an infrared and points out a third, extremely weak blood sample. She leaves Greg with orders to check up on the third sample. Down the hall at ballistics, Gil and Nicky learns that the rifle found at the scene was indeed the murder weapon. They also found a print on the rifle: Ananda's.

Ananda explains: "I entered through the back. The rifle was on my desk. I walked into the prayer room to ask my brothers about the gun. I returned to my office, placed the weapon outside, and went for help." Nicky informs him that tampering with the evidence is against the law; Ananda replies, "The temple is a holy place. Please understand: I was adhering to my teachings." Gil then asks if his teachings allow him to keep porn, and Ananda says: someone left the magazine at the temple. I kept it, in case this person came back. He also explains that if one is no longer attached to seeking pleasure, then pictures of naked women mean no more than pictures of waterfalls. Monks abstain from erotic behavior not because they believe sex is sinful, but because preoccupation with worldly pleasure diverts us from the path.

Now for the twist in the B plot: Ecklie, the investigator on the Watson case fifteen years ago, is annoyed because he just signed off on an authorization to destroy evidence. Catherine gives him attitude and points out that there was a glove at the crime scene. It wasn't photographed at the scene, but logged by Jimmy a few days after the murder.

Meanwhile, Sara and Gil study the prints on the rifle. The placement of Ananda's prints lead him to believe he didn't finger the trigger. It looks instead as though Ananda held the rifle by the stock, barrel down. Since Nevada doesn't require anyone to register rifles, the rest of the state's population is still a potential suspect. So this didn't help much.

The chewing gum Sara found is currently with Greg in the DNA lab so that he can extract DNA. Downstairs, Nicky points to a chunk of prayer room wall and explains to Gil that the presence of the place is somewhat odd. Gil doesn't see where he's coming from: "Bangers tag homicides all the time." Nicky explains further with, "But after those German tourists were killed, the Snakebacks [Buddhist gang] were pretty much wiped out." Gil is still skeptical, and the bobbing and weaving continues until Nicky concludes that he's been looking at a false clue.

Gil, in the next scene, is in his office on the phone with someone from the Air Force. The Air Force guy explains that, post-9/11, geosynchronous satellites have been monitoring military institutions and their surrounding areas. The Buddhist temple is less than two miles from Nellis. Gil asks if they can take a look. We then see the satellites at work, zooming in on the area around the temple and a license plate reflected in the hood of a car.

The license plate is a vanity plate that reads PROUD US. This was the only vehicle to pass through the temple gate, and it is registered to a Peter Hutchins. Gil sends Sara off, warrant in hand, to go process the truck. He and Nicky head into the coffee shop to interview Peter.

Gil makes small talk with the guy behind the counter, telling him that he heard some of the local business owners weren't happy with the members of the temple. The barista nods and says "They don't speak English and that bothered the other customers. And it was kind of hard to sell beer, or sandwiches, or videos when monks don't partake of any of those things," Pete explains. An old man at the counter offered his opinion: "Those monks changed the whole feel of this neighborhood. I'm not surprised at any of those murders." Gil asks for introductions; we learn this is Peter Hutchins Sr., and Mr. Hutchins Sr. Hutchins Sr continues: "I've owned this shop for twenty years. All of a sudden, these holy rollers move in here and business takes a nose-dive. I don't care what they say, it doesn't have a damn thing to do with the economy. Good night, Las Vegas. Good morning, Viet Nam." Just then Sara enters with prayer beads found in the PROUD US vehicle. The truck, as it turns out, belongs to Hutchins Sr. He immediately asks what Sara is doing in his truck, and Gil tells him about the government surveillance photos that picked up his truck at the temple during the murders.

At the B plot, Catherine goes to the place where she used to strip, waiting for Jimmy to meet her there. We learn about Catherine's special relationship with Jimmy—he "delivered her a whole new life" . Together, the two of them check out the fifteen-years-dead crime scene. Jimmy seems passionate about the victim, proclaiming that the day Stephanie was killed was the worst day of his life. Catherine then walks Jimmy through the crime scene. She asks him where the glove fits in the story, and when it fails to fit neatly, and asks him about the fact that it was discovered later. Jimmy gets angry and accuses her of accusing him of planting evidence, and stomps off.

Meanwhile, Nicky rains on everyone's parades when he informs the group that Hutchins Sr. was in Laughlin with the wife during the murders, and his alibi checks out. They absorb this news and Greg returns with the results of his tests: the blue substance found on a statue was paintball paint.

At the local paintball center, Nicky, Gil, and Sara have pried Hutchins Jr. away from his game. Sara studies Hutchins Jr.'s boot prints and mentally compares it to the ones she lifted, and Gil points out that with Dad in Laughlin and the truck at the crime scene, the evidence is pointing to Hutchins Jr. knowing something about the murders. Having matched the boot prints, Sara asks, "You were there, weren't you?" He is dragged into the interrogation fishbowl with his father and tells a story about how he and his friends visited the monastery for kicks a few weeks before the murders. Gil tells him that his boot print suggests he made his visit more recently. Junior falters and then says he was a week ago, but Tommy, his friend, took a statue. Junior went to give it back and was removing my boots when I looked inside, and saw them laying there. He says wanted to call the police, but knew if they found him there, they would think he was guilty. Gil asks how he knew to take of his shoes. "They were my friends." Hutchins Senior is not pleased with this, and does not take this well. Junior elaborates: "Someone once asked the Buddha, 'How do we escape the heat of a summer's day?' And the Buddha said, 'Why not leap into a blazing furnace?'"

Back at the B plot, Warrick's isolated another blood sample on the glove as well as human saliva. There was also saliva on the weapon. Catherine asks, "Well, how did blood from Kelso's mouth end up on the glove as well as the knife?" She pauses and then wonders if it was planted.

She then accuses her old pal Jimmy of planting evidence. He takes issue with her phrasing and feels that a more accurate description of his participation was to help the evidence along. She asks for Jimmy's blood because they isolated male blood on the murder weapon that does not belong to Kelso. Jimmy is predictably indignant and Catherine reveals that Jimmy was in love with Stephanie and she had rejected his proposal for marriage. This makes Jimmy pretty angry and he says if she wants his blood, she'll need a warrant.

In the next scene, Warrick delivers the envelope with results of Jimmy's DNA sample compared to the one on the knife. The blood sample is a total mystery, not matching anyone in CODIS, and therefore she's going to conclude that not only did Stephanie's real killer get away, Kelso served a lifetime sentence for a crime he didn't commit. In the interrogation tank, Catherine calls him on this and tells him she'll have to turn him in. He freaks out—he could not only lose his job, but get a heavy jail sentence, and plus Kelso was scum. Of course, he also reminds her that he rescued her from dancing, which is a hop step and a jump for turning tricks. She stands her ground, and turns Jimmy in.

The next scene is of Ananda walking the streets of Vegas. As Ananda gets to a crosswalk, Gil pulls up and says, "If you see the Buddha on the side of the road, kill him." Ananda replies, "Because the true Buddha is inside of us, so that is the false Buddha. Or a tired monk who doesn't drive because he can't control his anger." They laugh. Ananda gets in the car and Gil informs Ananda that both generations of Hutchins men are not the culprit. Gil then tells him about chewing gum -- Greg found traces of curry and saffron in the gum -- and Ananda reveals that the monks ate curry and saffron for dinner.

They go to the kitchen where Gil determines that the five monks ate together. Before they are able to get to the details of dinner, O'Reilly barges in and accuses Ananda of embezzling a thousand dollars from the school fund because bank records show a deposit of twelve thousand dollars instead of the thirteen thousand the monks raised. Gil notices that the account was opened the same day as the murders, and asks Ananda where the money was before that. It was in a box, in Ananda's office. They track down the carved-wood box, now empty, and upon opening it, notice a small pile of curry powder at the bottom. "Curry powder! Your temple employs a part-time cook!" he exclaims. Ananda says: "Mr. Suddahara moved on." Gil asks, "After you caught him with his hand in the till? Why didn't you tell us about Mr. Suddahara before?" Ananda replies that just because a man steals doesn't mean he kills. After the confession, Gil asks David Suddahara, "I'm curious about one thing: why did you shoot them in the sixth chakra?" It was an accident. He just shot them between the eyes.

As Gil exits the temple, he sees Hutchins Jr in meditation with Ananda. In cold storage, Catherine's pulling down the box of Stephanie's evidence, writing on the side, "Do not destroy. Case unsolved."

Chasing the Bus

A tour bus is bound for Vegas, forty miles outside of its borders, when a man staggers out of the bathroom in the back of the bus, holding a bottle of liquor. He heads down the aisle towards the front of the bus and sits behind the driver, offering him a sip. The driver demurs, telling him he knows his limits. Just then, he wheel begins shaking violently as a tire goes flat and the bus begins swerving, and then veers into a concrete barrier, off the edge of the road, and down a cliff.

The entire team arrives shortly thereafter, and looks down the cliff at the bus. It's on its side, a car pinned beneath it, and rescue people lay out body bags, and tend to the wounded. Sara comments, "I feel so useless." Gil says, right before the credits roll: "They do their job, and we do ours."

Some time passes before Gil starts barking orders. He wants cones, pictures of skid marks and loose asphalt, and anything they can even remotely regard as evidence. He also orders them to call in CSI Vegas cadets and support personnel to help. They scatter. Nicky heads to the wreckage and asks the only rescue doctor to point out the driver.

He's alive, sitting up and slightly dazed, covered with blood, relatively unharmed as he's the only person on the bus that was required by law to wear a seat belt. Just then, Greg arrives at the scene, eager to help, since there was a blanket call for assistance. Gil flatly refuses as he's not CSI personnel, but finally relents, and orders him to tag along with Warrick, who in turn is ordered to make sure Greg doesn't screw anything up or contaminate anything. Once Gil leaves, Nicky tells Greg that he'll be taking Nicky's notes.

Meanwhile, Brass has been talking to the bus company owner, Larry Maddox. As usual, Brass fills the role of expositor, telling Catherine: "He coughed up the passenger manifest, including the driver, Martin Draper. Twenty-four passengers, one PAL." PAL means Parolee At Large, one Calvin McBride, recently of the California State Penitentiary, convicted of aggravated assault. He was in seat 1-C. The fact that he was illegally crossing state lines was news to his parole officer.

Down at the scene, Catherine and Gil meet over by the bus; he says he thinks he knows why the bus pulled to the right. He shines his light on the tire blowout and notes that the other tire is still intact. Gil muses, "Newton's Third Law: For every action, there is an equal and opposite reaction. Tire to rim. Rim to axle. Axle to suspension. Suspension to frame. And the lower radius rod arm, which connects the axle to the frame..." Apparently, the lower radius rod arm, whatever that is, had snapped. They opine that it broke, causing the driver to veer to the left, thereby putting pressure on the right front tire, which caused it to blow and go off the road.

Catherine turns away to check out the Camaro pinned under the bus. The passenger, who was thought to be dead, is actually alive, his hand extended out the window, grabbing frantically at the air. Catherine grabs his hand in hers, telling him she'll get him out of there, and shouts for rescue. He is eventually freed from his wreck of a car and put in an ambulance. Catherine realizes her hands are covered in blood.

Meanwhile, Greg and Nicky are talking to Draper, who's saying that the wheel shook out of his hands. Nicky asks him when the wheel shook out of his hands. The driver sort of rambles about how they always stop at the McDonald's in Barstow. Nicky asks if he's ok and he just says, "No, we're behind schedule. I gotta get back to the bus." Draper tries to rise, but Nicky asks if he's had anything to drink. Draper says nothing, and then struggles to say, "I gotta...I gotta go." Nicky fetches a breathalyzer, but as Draper tries to exhale, he ends up coughing up blood. Nicky holds the driver so he doesn't collapse and orders Greg to get help.

He stands unmoving. Nick shouts his name a couple more times but Greg just stands there frozen. After the commercial break, Nick is telling Greg to quit apologizing—he just hasn't had training and simply isn't qualified. Greg says that he was upset by the blood: "Pre-collection, it's so different." Nicky says, "I remember my first time in the field. CSI-1, green as could be. Initial call was a robbery. I get there -- triple homicide. Blood all over the place. Mother and two kids." Greg asks how he dealt with it and Nicky responded simply, "You just do."

They then report to Gil, who tells them that they are missing one passenger: the ex con, Calvin McBride. He wasn't admitted to the hospital, and he's not in any of the body bags. Nick decides to check inside the bus. He walks along the windows since the bus is on its side, and shines his flashlight on the various personal effects, and blood.

Nick extricates himself from the bus and tells Gil and Greg what he found—the bottle of alcohol that the unshaven man was drinking. Gil bids Greg to bag the bottle to be tested for DNA. Nicky notes, "Seat 1C was the only seat with an unobstructed path through the windshield." Gil begins looking around, then asks Nicky, "Where's the other half of this windshield?" He and Gil begin looking for the glass and eventually find a pane of glass with the usual spider-web pattern of cracks, and a huge splotch of dark blood at the center of the web. Just a few feet further, Calvin McBride is on his back.

Meanwhile, Catherine has gone to the hospital to check after the Camaro driver, but she is facing some challenges because she doesn't know his name. She then sees him being wheeled into surgery and manages to ask him his name before he disappears into the ER. He says: "Eric. I just wanted to surprise her, that's all. If I don't make it, please tell her I'm sorry.

Daylight breaks and Gil is till at the scene, telling his underlings that he needs the two front wheels: axles, suspension, all of it. He then turns to do something else, and is distracted by a non-official person at the scene of the crime. She sniffles that he's on the bus, and he asks her why she's here. She breaks down crying.

On the stretch of road leading to the accident, Sara is slowly moving along the pavement collecting evidence, and Warrick is taking photos of the skid marks along the concrete barriers. She laments that since the highway is so heavily trafficked, there's a lot of stuff on the road that has nothing to do with the accident. Then she sees the second set of skid marks – the ones for the Camaro. Warrick muses that Gil had said that the broken rod arm caused the bus to waver. He opines that when the road arm hit the pavement, it left an impression on the road. Sara joins him in the reconstruction of the scenario, and agrees with him, theorizing that it crossed the highway, bounces off the K-rail, crossed four lanes of traffic, and somehow only took out the one car behind it.

Back at the CSI lab, Greg has figured out that the whiskey bottle was the ex-cons; the driver's DNA was not on it. In the morgue, Nick discusses the accident with the coroner, who tells him that the driver was probably disoriented not from alcohol, but from diabetes. He hadn't eaten anything in six hours, and became disoriented from hypoglycemia. Draper then died from massive injuries and internal bleeding.

Still on the scene, Warrick and Sara find a bolt that looks as though it's been cut or sheared. At the lab, Nick has learned that the vehicle was serviced the week before the crash and was in perfect condition. Just then, Warrick and Sara come in announce that they've got a three-quarter-inch bolt with a hex head that says it's a grade eight, but testing revealed that it's grade 5, which makes it softer than an 8. Gil notes that inferior bolts would cause the suspension to give, thus forcing the bus to veer all over the road, but Warrick interrupts Gil and says "No, the bolt snapped halfway through the skid, after the bus hit the K-rail." They can tell from the gouge in the road.

At the hospital, Catherine learns that the man in the Camaro didn't make it. His name is, or rather, was Eric Kevlin and he was a resident at the UCLA Medical Center; he was driving to Vegas to surprise his girlfriend. Apparently Kevlin, age thirty two, signed a pre-op Do Not Resuscitate order (DNR). Brass doesn't think it makes sense for a young person to have done so.

At the garage of the bus company, Warrick talks to the owner, Maddox, who laments that until last night, they had a perfect safety record. He says, "Accidents are inevitable," and Gil counters "Criminal acts, however, are not." This puts Maddox on the defensive and he rattles off the list of safety precautions his company takes: "I screen all my drivers, zero tolerance for drugs or alcohol, I keep strict maintenance records, vehicle inspection every forty-five days as required by law. You're not going to find anything criminal here." Gil hands him the sheared bolt. Maddox says that he buys all his parts from reputable vendors. This one came from a Brillway Bolt Company—Maddox says he'd just switched because they had a lower bid. Realizing he just jumped over a dollar to pick up a quarter, he grounds the fleet so they can remove all of the faulty bolts.

Sara matches rubber scraps taken from the road to the camaro and the bus. Brass questions people at the rest station in Barstow. A gas-station attendant reports that

Marty Draper was a regular; another attendant also noted a fight between a couple. Brass then talks to a mechanic who knows the details of the route traversed by the bus; he did not notice the couple fighting.

Back at CSI, Nicky and Catherine manage to squeeze into the wreckage of the Camaro and find the man's wallet. There are many, many pictures of the girlfriend in the wallet. Nicky recognizes the girl from the scene of the accident.

They then make a beeline for the girlfriend, who was on the bus, and is now in bed, resting to recover from her injuries. The girl says she knows that her boyfriend was going to surprise her, and that she was indeed surprised when he showed up in Barstow and told her he'd crashed her girls' weekend. We go to flashback, where the woman is yelling at Eric for being possessive and needy, and not giving her space. Catherine and Nicky move on and ask about the DNR, and it's because he was a doctor and saw people hooked up to machines, doomed for the rest of their lives to lie in a hospital bed. He swore he wouldn't want anyone he loved to go through that.

Back at the Lab, Gil is reviewing photos of the asphalt, looking for the dent in the road that would indicate the snapped rod so he could piece together the sequence of events. Sara paces around in the lab waiting for Greg to give her results. And she finally gets them.

She immediately runs to tell Gil: "I finally know the first action that initiated this skid. The right front tire came apart. When it blew, it left an indentation in the pavement...the treads from the right rear tire obscured it. The driver overcorrects, but since there's no more tire, all that force is displaced on the suspension system. The bolt snaps, the rod arm breaks, and the bus broadsides the Camaro." Anticipating Gil's question, she then says: "Why did the tire come apart in the first place?" Gil looks a forlorn: "I don't know." Sara practically shrieks: "I do. Chloroform inside the tire." She hands over the lab results for Gil.

The chloroform was an act of sabotage, and whoever did it used chloroform because it destroys the elasticity of rubber. The CSI's then set up a giant treadmill with a bus tire to figure out how long a tire would last after getting doused with chloroform. When Sara sets it up they notice that she had to touch the rim of the tire so she prints the rim of the bus tire to see if the perp had done the same. Gil's suspicious of Eric's girlfriend Tracy, or, alternatively, think that Eric may have sabotaged the tire in Barstow. Catherine runs off to check the Camaro for chloroform. .

Later, Sara's dusted and found a match for Sean Nolan, a former bus driver. The tire on the treadmill explodes, and everyone concludes that the tire was sabotaged in Barstow. Warrick visits Maddox and learns that Maddox fired Nolan for having pot in his locker.

Now, Nolan has been working in Barstow for two months and three of Maddox's buses have had blowouts in that time, all of which have gone through Barstow, and only one of which had the faulty bolt.

The three CSIs then head over to Nolan, and confirm he's the culprit when they use a hand-held detector to pick up traces of chloroform on a tire gauge. Nolan confesses, saying he did this in revenge. He had figured that even if the tires blew, the suspension system would hold. He is arrested, and charged with multiple counts of manslaughter.

Stalker

A phone rings in a house in the suburban outskirts of Vegas, and a mechanized male voice says, "No one is available. Please leave a message." The caller does: "Jane, you there? Pick up. Okay...I'll call back later." The camera pans back and we see that the answering machine is on a table in a hallway, and it holds 64 messages. Then we see Jane. She's crouched on the floor, clutching a baseball bat and sobbing in fear as she listens to the message. The phone rings again and Jane starts crying. The message plays again; this time, the same male voice hisses, "Slut. You can't hide from me, bitch." The message continues, "Jane, you there?" We see three deadbolts on the door. Still, the voice persists as Jane cowers, chewing on her fingers in nervousness: "Now, didn't I tell you not to bite your nails?"

Terrified, Jane pulls out the answering machine's power cord, dashes down the hall, closes her bedroom door, then hides in the closet. The bedroom door opens; her little dog comes over to the door, whimpering, and she pulls him into the closet, cuddling him close. She backs into a corner of the closet, and backs right against her black-gloved attacker. Jane has time to scream, and the attacker wrestles her to the ground.

The CSI's have arrived in the next scene. Catherine takes photos of Jane slumped over a toilet and concludes that she was posed. Jane, by the way, was blond in the first scene and is now a redhead. Gil and Catherine look at the tub, which is sullied with streaks of hair dye. Gil wonders aloud "Her hair's still wet. Do you think the assailant surprised her while she was dying her hair?" Catherine asks who called in the dead body; Gil responds that a neighbor heard the dog yelping and subsequently called the police. Catherine continues to look around the bathroom and sees that the bathroom window is nailed shut.

As Catherine and Gil walk down the hall, Gil also wonders what became of the dog. Catherine notes the triple door locks, the drawn shades, the alarm system. She tells Gil, "As far as we know, her place was perfectly hermetically sealed until the cops batter-rammed their way in." Catherine wants to know how he got in, and Gil is more interested in how he got out.

The credits roll and the next scene is of Nick, visibly upset, and looking down at Jane. Gil notices, and asks: "You've been staring at this girl for ten minutes. Do you know her?" Nick does not. He is instructed to help Catherine in the bedroom, and joins her just in time to see Catherine running an ALS over the comforter. Nicky hands Catherine tweezers, and she comes up with a thick, light-colored fiber. Nicky ducks under the bed and finds a plastic shopping bag with a red smudge in it. Gil sends Nicky off to fume the bag and to recruit Warrick and Sara.

Cut to the lab. As he roams through the hallways he notices a newspaper clipping on the wall: The headline says, "CRIME STOPPER: Nick Stokes." Nicky sighs and rips the paper off. Then he heads into the break room, where his colleagues are reading the article aloud and laughing. He handles it gracefully and tells them what Gil wants them to do. Warrick is to examine the blond hair collected from the scene, Sara is to look through phone records.

At the morgue, the coroner tells Catherine and Gil about the victim: Jane Galloway died from suffocation, and she's a natural blonde. Gil notes that Jane may have been suffocated, but there's no sign of strangulation. The coroner replies, "If she had struggled with her assailant, that effort alone could have limited her oxygen intake, causing further O_2 depletion of the brain." We establish that the attacker murdered and posed Jane, but declined to either rob or rape her..

Meanwhile, Nick tracks down Greg, having learned that he was the one who tacked the article to the wall and distributed copies to the other CSI's. He tells Greg to knock it off with the articles. Greg rebuts," You are the one doing the 'forensic spotlight' in the department newsletter." Nick looks pissed and says: "I didn't do anything, man. Someone from the community wrote a letter of commendation, Public Affairs ran it. Cool?" Greg nods. They then turn to work as if nothing happened.

It turns out that Jane had a temporary restraining order against her ex-boyfriend, Red, who, as it turns out, had called Jane thirteen times on the day of her murder Brass points out that this is thirteen more times than the restraining order permits. Brass and Sara run off to interview Red. They find him in his car, parked across the street from his house. Sara and Brass walk over to the car. He is covered in blood and slumped over the wheel of his vehicle. Sara calls for backup and goes for her gun. Then Red starts. Brass leads him over to the grass and they establish that although he's covered in blood, it's not his. He does not, however, remember getting the blood on him. He is taken to the interrogation tank.

Later that evening, Nick goes home from work, and we see how and where he lives. He has a big-screen television and lots of books. Nicky logs on to Internet Online, and sees that he has mail from someone named Horndog. Apparently, he went to the prom with Horndog, and she's sent photos. We see her partying and drunk, and then slumped over the toilet, passed out, in the same pose as Jane Galloway.

Nick then calls her and she explains that she was cleaning out the attic one day, stumbled upon them, and thought she'd send them to me for a laugh. Clearly creeped out, he tells Warrick about this at work. Warrick, of course, wonders if Horndog is a suspect. Nicky says she lives in Maine and has three kids. But he is clearly still creeped out about the similarities between those pictures and Jane's pose.

The next scene: Gil and Brass are walking down the hall, and Brass, as usual, exposits. They are on their way to meet someone who says he had a vision right before Jane Galloway's murder hours before it happened. Apparently, he produced details that weren't on the news or in the press release. When they meet him in the lobby, Gil says: "Captain Brass tells me you had some sort of vision about Jane Galloway's murder?" The man, Pearson then says: "I did...screaming face in a plastic womb. Blood shower. Three hearts beating very fast, two large, one small. Gil turns to go, asking Brass "This is your eyewitness?" when Pearson calls out, "The dog didn't make it, did it?" This seems to convince Gil.

Somewhere else in CSI central, Catherine and Sara are discussing Jane: in the last three weeks, she quit her job, she got subscriptions for Valium and Librium, she bought locks and alarms and other home-security devices. Sara sums it up, "Make no mistake: Jane Galloway was being stalked. Emotional terrorism at its finest. Here's the, uh, worst part. I ran a phone check on all her incoming calls. Guess where they were coming from." Catherine views the log and says, "Inside her house."

Back in the room with the psychic, Brass is telling Gil that Pearson happened to be at the Monaco Hotel the night Jane was murdered. In the next scene, Gil, Brass, and Pearson are standing in a hotel room in the Monaco and Pearson says, "I didn't know she was your victim." Brass tells us, "According to the front desk, you placed a call to Jane Galloway's room at 9:12 PM? Lasted twenty-one seconds?" Pearson says they talked energy. We see it all go down in a flashback. He says: "I'm calling from the next room. I don't mean to alarm you, but I'm feeling some serious negative energy coming from your room." Jane slams down the phone. Gil notes that Jane got three calls -- all from Pearson -- and shortly after Jane left the hotel that night, creeped out by the phone calls no doubt, Pearson also checked out. Gil wants to know why. Pearson says, "Well, she was suffering. And I shared her fear. It seems my intuition was accurate, as it turns out...I was only hoping to comfort her. I'm bound by that obligation." Gil wants to know if Pearson has any other crime-related visions. He says: "Three locks...hanging ghosts, hanging ghosts, chest to back, chest to back, A-frames, wooden beams, church dark." Well. That sure sheds a lot of light on a lot of things, no?

Back at Jane's house, Gil is showing Pearson around. He closes the front door, then asks, if Pearson was referring to the three locks on the front door. Pearson confirms that he was, but that he saw them at a much different angle, almost as if someone was looking down when viewing them. Gil and Pearson then walk over to a closet; we learn that this is what Pearson saw, only from above. Gil looks up at the top of the closet and notices a crawl-space entrance to Jane's attic. In the attic, there are holes drilled into the ceiling and labeled with the room location. Up in the attic, Gil calls Catherine on her cell phone and bids her to pick a number between two and five, then hold up her hand and display what number she picked. So Catherine does, holding up four fingers and looking around the empty room. Gil says: "Four. Thank you." He then shares with her the secret of Jane's stalker -- the bedroom closet had a door to the attic. Gil then uses the stalker's phone-tapping equipment to call Warrick and tell him that the blonde fiber is not hair; it's insulation.

Catherine comes up to see the Stalker Attic. Apparently he tapped into her second line and has labeled peepholes for every room in the house. Gil also introduced Mr. Pearson as "our psychic." Catherine just nods. Gil theorizes, "You know, I don't think this thing was about sex at all. I think it was about control. Voyeurism. Jane was like his, uh, little goldfish." Catherine wonders why the stalker left his digital camera with fiber-optic lens, night-vision goggles, and digital recorder in the attic. They also wonder, more importantly, how it got in. Gil thinks it's possible that at some point, Jane let him in. Catherine wonders, "Who do we let into our homes every day?" says, "If you've got a uniform on, you can walk through the front door." Catherine figures that the team can go through Jane's bills and see which utilities came to her house.

After interviewing a plethora of utility people in a montage to indicate the passing of time, we see Nicky and Warrick walk up to a house with a cable van in the driveway. Nicky immediately gets excited and says, "Luna Cable! Good company -- same as mine. A hundred and fifty channels!" They knock on the door. There is no answer so Nicky opens the unlocked door and calls out, "Mr. Crane?" Just then, Warrick's cell phone rings. To get better reception, Warrick heads back down the stairs, leaving Nicky to enter the house all by himself. As Nicky goes inside the near-empty house . Warrick turns his back to the door and says into the phone, "I can hardly hear you. We're at the satellite guy's house that installed Jane's cable." Nicky, meanwhile, notices a trail of dark red splotches. He whips out the latex gloves and opens the kitchen cabinet where the trail ends. As Nicky continues to look for the source of the trail, the camera zooms over to the pantry, where someone is silently crouching. Just as Nicky finds a pair of latex gloves covered in hair dye, he hears a noise and looks up.

We see Warrick still gabbing on the phone and then hear glass break. Warrick turns his head just in time to see Nicky go sailing out the window. He shouts, "Nick!" -- and pulls his gun before heading into the house. Then he immediately runs back out, pulling out his walkie-talkie to ask for immediate backup and emergency medical assistance.

After the commercial break, Nicky lies unmoving in a hospital bed, suffering from a concussion, two cracked ribs, a sprained wrist, and a laceration on his forehead. Warrick immediately begins blaming himself but Gil says, "You helped out Nick. That was the right thing to do." Catherine points out that Nick was alone and the stalker could have killed him, but didn't. Gil and Catherine go to check out the house again, and leave Sara and Warrick to see to Nick at the hospital.

Back at the cable guy's house, we find out that it belongs to one Nigel Crane, age 37, a cable company employee for eleven years. Somehow, Catherine and Gil have entered the house again, and are wandering around in the dark. There is no furniture, just a computer and a chair. Gil wanders off into the kitchen. He heads toward the pantry, flips on the light, and notices the door to the crawl space. He pulls himself up into the dark attic. It is contains Crane's extensive video library and his video camera, as well as furniture and other day-to-day objects.

Gil pops out of the crawlspace and excitedly says, "He lives up there! Not down here. Works, sleeps, changes his clothes, everything in the attic. He looks down on the world, separating himself from others. Fascinating, really." Catherine too looks excited and shows Gil the gloves she found, covered with hair dye.

They decide to watch Nigel's video library. The first tape focuses on the tourists that frequent the strip. Nigel's voiceover narrates with: "Walking pukes. Soulless, lost, useless, sick puppets. Little sheep looking for direction. Gullible. From an airplane, they used to look like ants. And now...they're all ants, all the time. You squash one."
The next one we watch them watch is night-goggle footage of Jane Galloway sleeping as Nigel says, "I see you, Jane." Sara and Warrick come in, apprise Gil and Catherine of

Nicky's condition (he's been released and told not to work) and settle into watching more videos. Catherine looks back over at the film and notices something, and everyone looks up to see Nicky's face, circled in red pen. Catherine says, "That's our crime-stopper article." Gil asks, "Isn't our newsletter in-house only?"

Warrick muses, "He may know him well enough to read his email." Sara wonders if Nigel did indeed manage to hack into Nicky's email somehow, and then pose Nick like the prom date. Gil wonders: "Why would he do that? Why Nick?" Well, why Jane? I guess it's easier to understand a woman being stalked and murdered, huh.

They skip ahead to more recent tapes and get the answer to the "Why Nick" question. Nigel explains: "It's like, he's, he's the kind of guy I always wanted to, um, to be. And, and that's why it's so great, because we're friends now. I feel like I can count on him, you know? I-I think if it came down to it, he would lay down his life for me. Ask him. Ask-ask Nick. Nick. Would you let me stop your heart?"

The next shot is of Nick taking his Vicodin. There's a knock on the door, and it's Pearson, saying, "My name is Pearson. Morris Pearson. We haven't met. I worked with Mr. Grissom on the Jane Galloway case." It's one a.m. but Nick lets him in anyway. He has had more visions. The first was of Nicky's address. Then Pearson says, "I see falling and crashing, somebody seeing through the back of his head. I don't know. I don't know. Green tea! Green tea! Does that mean anything to you? Green tea." He is interrupted when Nicky's phone rings. Gil says, "He's been in your house." He explains that Nigel Crane's been to Nicky's house and Brass is coming over with two uniforms to keep Nicky company; Nicky replies that the psychic is already keeping company. Gil tells Nicky to keep Pearson there, which would seem easy enough, but Pearson has disappeared.

So Nicky pulls a gun from a drawer in a hall table moments before Pearson (dead) and Nigel (alive) crash through the ceiling and land on a rug with a green T in the center. Nicky is so surprised to see a dead guy and a stalker fall through the ceiling that he drops his gun. As he tries to go for it, Nigel says, "You gotta watch who you let in here. The guy was snooping all over the place." Nigel gets the gun first and says: "Smart move -- spare gun. Keeping it right by the phone, right? Near your address book and takeout menus." Nicky tells Nigel the cops are on the way and notices that Nigel's wearing his clothes. Curious-er and curious-er!

Nigel then goes into the speech killers give before placing victims in an easily-escapable situation involving an elaborate and exotic death: "I picked them up at the dry cleaners and I hope you don't mind, it's just that, I just get a little confused about what's yours and what's mine." Nicky asks Nigel, "When did we meet?" Nigel says: "Sports package. One hundred and fifty channels. I even threw in a few movies channels free. We talked for, like, forever. It's like I knew you my entire life. ..The minute I met you, I knew we connected, because you told me what you did, and I knew exactly what you were talking about, because that's what I do. I do it too. You know, I observe people. I notice everything about them. I watch them all the time." Nicky jumps in with: "Like you watched Jane Galloway?" Nigel continues, "Jane was cool. But it never would have worked out between us, you know. Never. I mean, she had a boyfriend, and she was kind of stuck-up. And you know what? She would have totally, totally gotten between us. So, you know, consider that...a gift." Nicky's struggling to follow the line of logic here. Nigel clarifies, "Prom night. Your date, Melissa. Bent over the toilet puking her guts out. Is that ringing any bells? You know, you mentioned her name in your sleep." He then points to Pearson and says "You want to open him up?" Nicky says "No, no. That's not my job. That's a coroner's gig. You should know that." Now Nigel starts to go sort of berserk. We Flash to Nicky passing Nigel as he read his mail, and when he went into the house with Warrick. Nigel begins screeching: "You are so self-absorbed. I was right in front of your face. Manners, Nick! MANNERS!" He points a gun at Nick's face and tries to tell him all about what a shot in the face does at close range. Nicky says, "I don't want to disappoint you, Nigel. But this isn't the first time I've had a gun in my face. How do you want this to end, Nigel?" He says he wants Nick to remember his name, and turns the gun on himself. The two men wrestle for the weapon, but then the black and whites arrive.

Nigel is then put in the interrogation tank, where he doesn't seem to be offering anything that's terribly helpful. He says over and over again "I am one and who am I?" There's a moment of silence as Nigel heads toward the one-way mirror. Sara says "Twenty-five years to life, Nick. It's over." Nick corrects her: "It's not over for me. It's over to Jane Galloway." The show ends with Nigel asking, "Who am I?"

Cats in the Cradle

The show begins with a cat meowing plaintively. The camera takes the p.o.v of the cat as it enters a suburban house and meets up with several other cats in a living room, where they meow together. The camera switches to an aerial shot and we see a passel of cats eating the body of an elderly woman.

In the next shot, CSI has arrived. We learn that the victim is one Ruth Elliott, eighty years old, and she had at least twenty cats. The mail was piling up, so the mailman looked in the window and called 911. O'Reilly cautions Catherine and Gil to take a deep breath before heading inside.

As Catherine and Gil enter the apartment, a cat caterwauls in the background. Catherine's eyes widen and she coughs, sputtering, "Oh, God. I didn't think anything could mask a decomp. The coroner arrives, struggling to maintain composure since he's allergic to cats. He gasps out that rigor mortis has passed, lividity is fixed, there's extensive marbling on Ruth's limbs, and she's been dead for three or four days. He then runs out of the house.

Gil and Catherine examine the body. She is pretty chewed up. As Gil and Catherine watch a cat being shoved in a cage, Catherine wonders if they turned on her. Gil notices a deep wound near the woman's heart. "This woman was stabbed," he says. "I guess the cats are off the hook." They notice a footprint on the floor; it looks as though it came from a woman's shoe. Catherine begins lifting the print.

She tells Gil that most of the prints are partials, from animal control officers' boots, but she's found a non boot print that suggests a high heel. There are no signs of forced entry or theft anywhere. As Warrick walks into her bedroom, he sees a lock in the closet wall. It hides a wall-safe—which is empty. Warrick notes this, then begins taking prints. He then shares this information with Catherine, who muses, "A high-heeled thief who knew exactly what to look for, and killed the only obstacle in their path."

Of course, there is a B plot. Nicky and Sara meet Brass by the shell of a burnt-out car that had exploded. The exploded BMW is driven by one Marcie and she's wrapped in a blanket, looking dazed as she gives her report to a police officer. We then meet Marcus Remick, an eyewitness. He's also talking to police officers.

They split up to conduct interviews and Sara is assigned to Marcie. She asks her what happened, and Marcie says that she was on her way to her father's office. On Thursdays, they have dinner and she helps him with his payroll. Her story is, of course, accompanied with flashback footage. We then see her noticing a weird sound coming from under the hood of her car, and driving it into the garage, where she tells Marcus that her car is making a really strange noise.

Then we turn to Marcus' conversation with Brass. He says: "Lady's driving a brand-new Beemer, first service is 15,000 miles. Things don't go wrong." He says he checked it out anyway because of how "women get". We see them open the hood to find ticking bomb, and then Marcus leading Marcie to safety. The car blows up.

Nicky and Sara look at the car together. Nicky notes that the bomb's detritus blew backward toward the driver. Maybe the bomber knew what he was doing, assuming Marcie was the intended target. And the only people who had access to the car were Marcie and her husband.

At the morgue, we learn that the cats started eating her after she was dead. Cause of death: cardiac trauma. She was stabbed lateral to the sternal border, just below the fifth intercostal space, straight into the right ventricle. The wound tract is slick, so its been swabbed and sent to Greg to investigate. Gil notes that Ruth's lungs were filled with fluid from a severe staph infection. The coroner dismisses this as irrelevant. Gil's cell phone rings, and when he answers it, he learns that there was a witness.

The witness was a child of a neighbor who we previously saw at the crime scene. The daughter, Jessica Trent, says, "The lady over there, the one that died, she was nice. She had cats. She let us play with them." Catherine asks Jessica to tell her what she told her mom, and the older sister Jackie pipes up: "I can. Jessica and I were playing handball against the garage door. We saw Mrs. Stein go into Mrs. Elliott's house, and they were yelling." Jessica chimes in with: "When Mrs. Stein came out, she looked really angry. Kind of like when Mommy's boyfriend is late for dinner. She hates that." Mrs. Stein, apparently, is a neighbor who had previously filed three nuisance complaints against the victim. As the adults are talking, we see Jessica lean in and whisper to Jackie, "Don't say anything." Catherine, with the eagle eye only a mother can have, asks the girls what's so secret, and Jessica whispers into her ear. The secret, as it turns out, is that Mrs. Stein hates cats.

At the lab, Sara and Nick check out debris from the car. They immediately conclude it's a pipe bomb with a cap at either end. Sara then picks a grommet out of the debris and launches into a lengthy explanation as to what purpose they serve. Brass then comes in and inquires as to their progress and he then informs us that Marcie's husband is the junior foreman at her father's company, Tobin C&D Incorporated.

Sara and Nicky, then head to Tobin C&D. They introduce themselves to Jonathan Claddon. We learn that just about everyone who works for C&D (which stands for construction and demolition) knows how to make a bomb. But he'd never blow up his wife. Sara points out that he didn't come to his wife's aid at the crime scene after her car blew off. They are interrupted by his father-in-law, who sends him off on some task or another. After Jonathon is safely out of earshot, the father-in-law says that he's cheating on Marcie, or hoping to.

At the lab, Greg has identified what was on the end caps in the car bomb: nitroglycerine, and sawdust. Meanwhile, Sara's analyzing the other end cap for screw thread pattern and fingerprints.

Cut to Nicky and Sara talking to Claddon, whose fingerprints, as it turned out, were on the end cap. He says: "My father-in-law's company is the largest purchaser of end caps in Nevada. I log inventory." Brass then notes that per the ATF, every stick of dynamite is catalogued. Claddon checked out a case of twenty-four sticks and only checked twenty-three in. He replies, "It was stolen. Look,

I'm the one who reported the theft. I kept the dynamite in my SUV, inside a storage magazine." Nicky asks if he is claiming that someone broke into his SUV and stole a stick of dynamite. Indeed he is. Brass switches then asks about his mistress, and Claddon denies having one, saying, "Marcie's the best thing to happen to me. Plus I've got an ulcer. Do you have any idea what an affair would do to me. I work my butt off for her old man. I barely have enough time to sleep, let alone Romeo some other girl. And the truth is, nothing I do is ever good enough. Tobin wouldn't even let Marcie take my name. Marcie handles the payroll and she has a rep for short-changing overtime. Talk about pissing people off. Any one of those guys could have put that bomb in her car." Hmmm. Very interesting. Sara asks him why he didn't share this information earlier. Claddon says that it isn't Marcie's fault that she's disliked; she does what daddy says.

Back at the cat infested house, Catherine presents neighbor Debbie Stein with a warrant for her shoes. In the lab, later, Warrick helps Catherine make prints off each shoe in the hopes of finding a match to the footprint in Ruth's house. They find a nice black wedge heel that matches and smells like cat urine.

Cut to Debbie being interviewed by Gil, saying that she was a pig with a stinky house and didn't belong in the neighborhood. Gil then asks why Debbie was in her house; Debbie responds, "I wanted to give her a chance to find homes for her cats before I called the humane society. To report her. By law, you can only own three." Catherine points out that a witness heard Debbie yelling at Ruth; Debbie says that Ruth was irrational. Back in the interrogation room, we find out that Debbie talked to Ruth about six days ago, before taking a trip to Los Angeles. After Debbie leaves, Catherine comments, "She had an answer for everything." They decide to check her alibi.

It checks out. They have lost their only suspect. They are cheered, however, when they identify the prints on the wall safe: they belong to Tyler Elliott, Ruth's son. His fingerprints are on file owing to the non-gaming work card he had so that he could work at the Tangiers.

In the next scene, Gil asks Tyler, "Your mother died and you never claimed the body. How come?" Tyler replies, "Funerals are expensive. I'm broke." As it turns out, he filed bankruptcy recently, and feels that no one would have showed up at her funeral anyway. O'Reilly asks, "So how often did you see her?" Tyler responds, "Twice a month. Went over, made sure bills got paid, brought her medication, stocked the fridge. All the stuff any good son is supposed to do." Catherine asks about the safe and he says that a month ago, one of her cats got locked inside and she couldn't remember the combo. So she called him for help. Tyler says hotly, "I didn't steal her money. She didn't have any. The only thing she had was the house, and she left that to some damn cat sanctuary." Here, he starts to get teary-eyed, saying he is broke and she left the house to cats.

Back in the B-plot, Marcie is claiming that "somebody put the wrong bomb in the wrong house because stranger things have happened!" Sara invites Marcie to talk alone but Marcie informs Sara that she and her husband have no secrets. Sara decides to spit it out and says: "Listen -- about your marriage. Your father said --" prompting Claddon to protest, "Your father ran his mouth about our personal life?" She admits that a few weeks ago she got the idea that William J. Macy was cheating her because he was never home and never interested, and then finishes with telling Sara "You shouldn't put too much stock in this because every couple has their problems." Sara watches the two stalk off, wondering why Marcie's so disinterested in finding out who sabotaged her car..

Unable to find the vise grip that was used to tighten the cap on the bomb, and unable to find anything of note with their warrants, Sara and Nicky revisit the wreckage of the car. He and Sara walk through the likely chain of events: the bomb was triggered to go off sixty seconds before detonation -- and the trigger that started the countdown was the latch on the car hood. They start wondering: how could a mechanic immediately spot a car bomb? And why would he close the lid on a bomb in a car?

Gil and Catherine pay a visit to the lab and learn that the slick substance in Ruth's wound tract was mineral oil. Greg theorizes that it came from an old knife; new ones are made with steel. At the cathouse Catherine and Gil ALS everything to find the murder weapon, to no avail. They pause and notice a little cat saunter by them and exit through the kitty door. They both think this is odd; animal control supposedly rounded up all the cats. They then proceed to follow that kitty straight across the street, where Jessica and her sister are playing with the cat, whom they've dubbed Rascal. Gil immediately notices the gaping wound on the cat's haunch. Gil asks if he can hold the cat but Jessica snaps "No. He doesn't like you." At around this time, their mother is approaching to call the girls to dinner and Gil raises the issue of Rascal's cut and offers to swab it, as the cat might need medical attention. Megan is dismissive and says, "It's just a cut. It'll heal." Gil tries another tact and says: "For your daughters' sake, wouldn't you rather be safe than sorry?" The cat gets swabbed. We later find out why Catherine swabbed the cat: it's got an open sore and a missing patch of fur -- both indicative of a staph infection.

Meanwhile, Sara and Nicky have tracked down Marcus the mechanic and in his garage is the vise grip that matches the one used to assemble the pipe bomb, though he claims that it belongs to a different mechanic.

Soon, Marcie is back in the interrogation room, asking why she would possibly want to put a pipe bomb in her own car. Brass says: because Nevada is a community property state, anything someone owns during a marriage is up for a fifty-fifty split during a divorce -- including the twenty-five percent of the Tobin C&D business that Marcie owns. If she and her husband were to divorce, Jason would become part owner of the company. But if he goes down for attempted murder, he goes to jail and she get to keep everything because a criminal can't profit from his own malfeasance. Nicky sharply adds that Marcie's prints are the ones on the vise grip. Eventually, Marcie says, "So what if I made a bomb. That's not a crime." We then find out that Marcie owed $20K in repairs on a Volvo, her dad kicked in another $30K, and for a mere $50K, Marcus's collusion was bought and sold. Marcie still doesn't get it. She says, "Look, I'm fine, and my husband is fine and it was my car that exploded, so does this really need to go any further?" Brass explains that since she and her dad were conspiring to frame her husband for attempted murder, he thinks it does, yes.

And now the A plot must come to a close. Gil and Catherine try to figure out how it is that Ruth and Rascal share the same staph infection when he's the Trents' cat and the Trent family does not have staph. They conclude that it's entirely possible that Rascal was originally Ruth's. After a brief visit to the Trent house -- where Catherine and an ALS light find a cracked novelty pen filled with mineral oil, then test it to confirm the presence of staphylococcus, the girls are dragged into the tank with Catherine. She holds up the pen and tells the girls, "We know that Mrs. Elliott was killed by this pen. Can one of you tell me what happened?" The advocate asks the girls if they understand what Catherine's asking. They say nothing and eventually Jessica says that "She didn't mean to do it. I'm sure she didn't." "she" apparently, is also known as "Mommy". We see a shot of Megan Gallagher watching the questioning with a shocked look on her face. Jessica says that the family went over to ask to adopt Rascal, Ruth refused, and Megan Gallagher sent the kids away with the cat and killed Ruth. As Jessica spits all this out, the other girl won't say anything. Catherine then asks, "Girls, do you know about fingerprints? When you touch something -- like this floaty pen, for instance -- you leave behind an invisible mark that's special, that's yours. I have a way to see these invisible marks, and we found these fingerprints on the pen. And they don't belong to an adult." Jackie finally speaks up: "They're not mine." Her sister rebuts that with

"Tattletales burn in hell." She then says, "The old lady should have just given me the cat. I lied before. She wasn't nice. She was mean." We see the real scene in flashback: the girls go over to ask if they can adopt Rascal, Ruth refuses gently, and Jessica flips out. She urges her sister to take the cat and run, then knocks Ruth over and stabs her with the floaty pen. This is all news to "Mommy". . She says, "I told the girls they could have a cat if Mrs. Elliott gave them one. I knew she never would -- that's why I made the promise." The last shot is of Jessica crying for her mommy.

Anatomy of a Lye

Somewhere in Vegas, children are frolicking gaily, laughing in the sun, playing the games that only children do. Then one trips and falls down. He immediately starts screaming: "The dirt burned my hands!" he wails, as his palms redden.

Sometimes after night has fallen, the child is getting his hand bandaged, and we see Sara, Brass, and Gil at the scene. Gil asks, "What's hazmat doing here?" Brass replies replies, "Kid's playing tag, takes a header in the dirt, ends up with first-degree burns on his hands... So hazmat arrives, figuring some chemical spill, starts removing the toxic soil, and bam -- a shovel slams into a shoulder blade."

Sara and Gil examine the body. Sara observes that the clothing's in shreds, and so is the body's epidermal tissue. Gil immediately concludes that someone doused the body in lye. Sara puts on a hazmat suit and jumps into the pit where the corpse was found. She finds the victim's wallet; the dead guy is a Nevada resident named Bob Martin, aged thirty-one. The twenty dollars in the wallet rules out robbery. Sara pokes around more and spots something in the dirt—a paint chip, or a flake of metal, and bags it.

In the morgue, we learn that flesh will bubble and hiss and liquefy if left in lye. The time of death was 24 hours ago. The dead man's shins that look like the result of a being hit by a car: "Comminuted fractures of the proximal third tib-fib, both legs. Bumper hits right below the knees. Sure sign he was hit by a car. This however, does not explain the bruising, which suggests that he survived the impact. In addition to his crushed shins, he has a ruptured patellar tendon, laceration of the saphenous vein, and multiple incised wounds containing slivers of glass. There are no arterial lacerations or underlying vessel damage, confirming the death was not immediate. It took the man 48 hours to die.

And now for the B plot. Off in the mountains surrounding Vegas, we learn a Bureau of Land Management chopper saw a body. The victim is twenty-six-year-old Las Vegas resident Stacy Warner. Nicky and Lockwood walk over to check out her body. on her back, in the middle of a bare patch of land. There is an engagement ring but no wedding band, a scrape on Warner's face, and when Nicky pries open her eyelid, the white of her eye is flooded with blood. "Orbital bone is fractured," he notes. At the corner of her mouth is a small down feather. Nicky tags the feather, notes the speck of blood and maggot in Warner's ear, and drops the maggot into a jar. After taking a soil sample from under the body, he takes off to get the maggot some beef jerky.

Back at the A plot, Gil and Sara pay a visit to Bob Martin's pad and meet his roommate. Apparently the roommate got divorced last year and Bob's wife kicked him out six months ago. The roommate says he is two months late on the rent, and how should he collect now that the collectee is dead? Sara and Brass exchange disgusted glances and then proceed with the interview. The two apparently worked at the Tangiers together and on Mondays, Martin would go off shift and walk over to "the university" and work in the darkroom before taking the bus home. Martin didn't come last Monday night but Martin was always breaking up and making up with his wife Charlotte. So the roommate thought nothing of it.

In the next scene, Gil and Sara flip through Martin's photos and note that all of them are the same woman. Gil stops in the middle of the road - and notes silver flecks on the pavement. Sara picks up a piece of plastic that looks like a headlight cover. Sara wonders, "Assuming this was a hit-and-run, how does a guy with two broken legs end up on the other side of town, buried in a park, covered in lye." Also puzzling is that there is no blood.

After the commercial break, Sara and Gil are in a large office, talking to a dislikable man named Weston. He assumes Gil and Sara are here to tell him that they've found the Mercedes which he reported missing last week. Sara asks to see a copy of his police report; Weston responds that he is a lawyer. Sara, awfully testy today, rebuts: "I didn't ask if you had sold your soul to the devil, I asked if you had a copy of the police report," she snaps. He then whips out the report. He says he stopped for take-out on Monday night and when he came out of the restaurant, it was gone. Gil asks, "Don't most of these luxury vehicles have security systems?" He then demands to know why they're asking so many questions. Gil tells him that they are investigating a hit and run, and Weston immediately asks if the person who stole his car hit someone. We find out that Weston will be working in criminal defense. Gil asks him if he remembers what clothes he wore yesterday, and he does: blue pinstripe, light-blue oxford, gray tie. Sara asks to see them and he produces the clothing, swaddled in plastic dry clean bags. She notices the oxford shirt has a few holes, then when Sara asks him to take off his shirt, because "lye can burn through fabric; it can also burn through skin." Weston says, "You want me to strip, you're going to need a warrant."

And now, the B plot. Warner, the woman found in the desert, died from drowning. Dry-drowning, to be precise.

The coroner elaborates: "Happens in about ten percent of all cases. When drowning occurs, the larynx closes involuntarily, preventing air and water from entering the lungs, resulting in hypoxia, a reduced concentration of oxygen in the blood, and ultimately ending in suffocation. Thus, water's kept out of the lungs -- dry drowning. In wet drowning, hypoxia also occurs, but the larynx relaxes and water floods the lungs. Still, the question remains: how does a girl drown in the middle of the desert?"

Nicky decides that the fiancée may have the answer to that question. In the next scene, Nick is interviewing the fiancée, and asking why he didn't file a missing persons report. He says: "As far as I knew, she was on her solo trek in Diablo, working on her NESTFs." "NESTFs-- National Extreme Sports Trainer Finals. I had mine last week. Did it in three days total, so I didn't expect her back for at least two more days." Nicky asks if he can have a look-see and Nicky immediately heads toward the pool and takes water samples. He also sees a tiny scrape of blood on the side of the pool, and swabs it. He asks the fiancée if he knows how the blood got there. He does not. Nicky asks if he knows how Stacy suffered head trauma; he does not, and vehemently asserts he would never hurt his fiancée. Nicky, however, is not having it: "No? Then how do you explain the domestic disturbance call to this address two weeks ago?...The neighbor who complained said you were really yelling at Stacy. Said it sounded abusive." Hudson says, "We're sports trainers. We say some really crazy things to get each other to do one more lap in the pool, one more crunch." In a flashback, Stacy's doing crunches while Hudson yells, "Are you a liar? Are you going to give me more? Are you weak? Are you worthless?" We get Hudson's alibi-- he was at the Big Sky triathlon -- and then the scene ends.

Back at the A plot, Brass explains to Sara and Gil that he found Weston's Mercedes based on a call from a tow guy named Sullivan. The tow-guy Noel, is explaining that the parts of an S-class Mercedes are worth four to five times the blue book value of the car. There's a healthy incentive for making sure that car gets stripped real quick-like. Brass asks if Noel knew the driver's name, but Noel does not, saying, "Someone throws you three hundred thou in used parts, the one response is 'Thank you very much.'" The parts are now strewn all over the shop. They tell Noel they need to collect the parts as part of their investigation.

Cut to Gil and Sara inspecting the seats in the lab. Sara sprays luminol and the seat practically glows in the dark. They conclude that the location of the blood on the seats and the dash indicates that the victim was inside the vehicle. Sara suggests that the driver hit Martin, stopped, and put him in the front seat. Gil wonders where they would have gone from there. Sara says she will send the car swabs for comparison with Martin's DNA.

In the next scene, Nicky's standing over a light table and looking at the pool and blood samples. The blood from the poolside matches the female victim, however, such a small amount of blood found in her own home isn't enough to prove anything. Nicky brings Warrick up to date on the fiancée and explains: "That muscle head boyfriend? He's a little shady. He's hiding something, I can feel it." Warrick picks up a sample baggie and notes that the item inside looks like basalt, and says: "You only find this rock at high altitudes like 4000 feet." The victim, however, was found at 1500 feet.

Meanwhile, Sara has learned that the blood in the car matches Martin's blood. They have also found visible blood drops under the passenger seat of the car, and the radiated spatter the blood drops made while falling. Catherine appears to look at the car parts and says, "So if this car were stolen, the ignition lock would be punched, right?" Sara looks down and tries to recover with, "We-we would have caught that."

They pay a visit to Weston, who explains it thus: "I was too embarrassed to tell you that I left my keys in a car that costs eighty thousand dollars, and I don't want my insurance company to know either." Sara once again asks him to take of his shirt, and when he refuses, she shows him her warrant. Weston says, "I can call Judge Scott, contest your grounds." Sara smiles and says, "You want to refuse? One of us will take it off you." Weston stands shirtless before everyone, and there is a large diagonal abrasion from where a seatbelt must have cut into his torso with considerable force. Brass says they have enough to get him on a hit and run, and Weston says: "Did I forget to mention that thudding noise I heard as I drove to get takeout?" Weston's quite convinced that his car was stolen, so he is in no way responsible for anything that the car may have done. Brass arrests him anyway, and escorts him out.

Meanwhile, in the mountains, Nick and Lockwood are trekking up to 4,000 ft. Lockwood notices a tattered down jacket hung up on a nearby crag of sandstone. It is, however, a men's extra large. Nicky rifles through the pockets and finds a printed ridge map. It's got an email header on it that says: to Matt Hudson, per his request for a trail map. Nicky says, "Maybe he left for his marathon a day later than he said he would. He followed her out here, they started arguing, no neighbors around to call the cops...she manages to fight her way free, finds higher ground, he follows her and takes her down." Lockwood is skeptical: "He drowns her with canteen water? I'll let you run that one by the D.A." Nicky tells Lockwood "You should try describing a scuba diver up a tree. This is nothing. Nah -- the evidence tells a story."

Hudson, however, insists that he gave Warner the jacket for night layering, as extreme hikers aren't allowed to carry bedrolls. Nicky sighs and says: "help us out here, man. I've got prior disturbance calls, her blood on the pool, her body drowned in the middle of the desert with your jacket nearby, your map." Hudson brightens when he hears about his map and asks for it back. Nicky says he can have it back when their investigation is complete. As they leave, Nicky's spirits are visibly buoyed: "He doesn't want me to have this map, and I want to know why."

At around this time, Sara and Gil learn that Weston made bail, and meet him in his driveway. Gil shows him the warrant and says that they will be starting in the garage. Weston does not handle this well. He tells Gil: "I'm filing a complaint with your supervisor. You're harassing me." Gil is not terribly broken up over the thought of this threat and says: "If you're a lawyer, you should know the legal definition of harassment. Investigating a crime doesn't quite fit that criteria. However, a false accusation of harassment within earshot of my colleagues can be construed as slander. I know the law too -- and I've actually been in a courtroom too."

That said, they enter the garage. There's a car inside, with splatters of caked, thick mud. Gil, remembering that he and Sara walked by a lot of sprinklers to get to this house said, "This was parked outside?" "Now that's a crime?" Weston says snarkily. Brass backs the car out of the garage to see what's underneath. There is a sparklingly clean patch of garage floor. Sara swabs the floor and finds evidence of blood.

At around this time, Nicky is hanging with Ronnie the document analyzer guy, telling him: "This guy was really nervous about me having this map." He can't however, tell Ronnie what to specifically look for. Ronnie says, "I'll test the components of the inks and then bombard the paper with different wavelengths of light. We'll see what's up."

Later, Nicky asks Gil about the maggot; Gil replies that it's from the family of sarcophagids but this maggot was exposed to a freezing temperature pre-pupation, and its growth was stunted. Nicky's protests that they found the victim in the desert and Gil surmises that it could have been a very cold night.

Slightly miffed, Nick heads to the computer lab. Greg immediately offers his opinion: "So I was thinking. To most people, Las Vegas means 'the Strip.' But it really means 'the meadows...Nevada is a basin-and-range state. Down in the desert basin, hardly any rain. Up in the mountain ranges, it's forty inches a year. That's more than Seattle. That's more than San Francisco. That's more than --" Nicky seems to see where he's going with it and remembers that there was great weather last week, but in Diablo, two days before the body was found, it was not so nice. "The mountain shadow effect," Greg concludes.

Elsewhere, Sara informs Gil that if you fill up a car with enough blood, it's going to begin to leak through the bottom. Sara begins imagining what happened: "The head of the victim crashed into the passenger side of the windshield...I'm thinking that the car clipped the victim here" – the shins -- "he was catapulted" -- she climbs on Ecklie's car to demonstrate -- "and was positioned something like this" – and lays on the windshield.

The victim's blood then dripped on the mat. Gil says that the victim could have been conscious until he lost a third of his circulating blood volume, so it's possible he was wedged into the windshield of Ben Weston's Mercedes, which was parked in Ben Weston's garage. Sara says" We know where Bob Martin was. Where was Ben Weston?" Sara then notes that the tow truck driver was very probably lying about the extent of the damage to the car.

We soon learn that Weston and Noel went to the same high school. Weston snitched on Noel during a prank, leading to Noel's felony conviction. After Brass threatens to make Noel an accessory to murder, Noel coughs up the details. He said that Weston unloaded the Mercedes under the guide of "making it up" to the guy whose life he ruined six years ago by snitching.

Over at Plot B, Nicky tells Lockwood what he has learned about the weather. It is summed thusly: In the shadow effect, the barometric pressure strikes down, the temperature strikes down , the humidity spikes up, and the warm air condenses. The mountains then get a flash flood. Nicky confirms that on the night Warner died, the mountains were showered with three inches of rain in twenty minutes. Nick theorizes that Warner was scaling a ridge when the rain hit. She slipped, caught herself, then got hit in the face with a gout of water. Since she was out of it from hitting her head, she couldn't fight the current effectively. She was drowned in the flood water and her body was carried to the base of the canyon. Nicky then gets a call from Ronnie: the map's been tampered with. They immediately confront the fiancée and tell him what they found: he made a meadow look like an impenetrable ridge, leading Warner to explore much more dangerous alternatives up the mountain. Lockwood says, "If she had a good map, she might have been able to find her way out of the highlands by nightfall." Hudson protests that he never meant for his fiancée to die; he only wanted her to have a worse race time than he did. He asks if he is being charged with her death and Lockwood tells him no: "You altered the map, but you didn't make it rain."

Weston, meanwhile, is in the tank, arguing that Gil and Sara's evidence is circumstantial and their physical evidence can be charitably described as pathetic. Gil then whips out Weston's cell phone and tells Weston that Noel found it in his car. There was one call made -- to 911, at 2:30 AM on Tuesday morning, while the car was still in is possession. They then play the tape; it's the victim pleading for help, but the cell phone location isn't logged, so no one can figure out where he is or how to rescue him. The operator tries to get information, but Martin is facing some challenges: he's stuck in the windshield of a garaged car. Sara angrily lectures him: "You know the law. You hit a guy. It was an accident. But you let it escalate -- first-degree murder. I spoke with your senior partner. It was your first day on the job. Big firm. Big welcome. How many drinks did you have that night?" Gil tag teams and jumps in: "Let me guess. You wanted the alcohol to wear off before you called it in, right? Have a cup of coffee, sober up, then call the cops? But unfortunately, Bob Martin woke up." In grainy flashback cam, we see Weston entering his garage, where Martin begs for help. Weston leaves and closes the door again. Gil continues: "What do you do now? You can't walk into the emergency room: 'Hey, this guy was bleeding to death in my garage while I was eating moo shu pork.'"

Just then, an officer summons Sara out of the tank, insisting it's relevant. It's the roommate. He hands Sara a piece of paper, and says he found it while packing up Bob's stuff, and he figured the CSIs would want it. She returns to the tank and hands the paper over to Gil. Gil looks at it and continues his diatribe: "When a driver hits a pedestrian, the presumption is, the driver is negligent. When a driver's been drinking and he hits a pedestrian, it's no longer negligence, it's reckless homicide. But when a pedestrian intentionally throws himself in front of a moving vehicle, the driver's no longer responsible. Legally, he's off the hook." Sara explains: "This suicide letter was written by Bob Martin to his wife Charlotte. When you hit him Monday night, it wasn't an accident. You were off the hook." Gil finishes, "Until you let him die". And there it ends.

Cross Jurisdiction

We begin the episode at a cocktail party at a mansion. Outside the window is a little girl, staring in. She sadly watches a few couples staggering across the lawn. Back inside, a young woman hangs all over a balding man and tells him "We should have these parties more than once a month," he replies, "I wouldn't want Mina to be jealous." The man notices a silhouetted figure standing in the doorway. Then four adults head into the bedroom for a ménage a catre.

Of course, this is when the little girl opens the door. She watches the drunk revelers head to the bedroom, then gets back into bed. The clock reads 12:20 AM. The next shot returns to the clock and it's 3:45 am. There are two gunshots. The girl creeps out of bed and opens the door. The man in the doorway is backlit so we don't see his features but the little girl does.

And then it's dawn, the black and whites arrive, and Brass is expositing: "Two days ago he had a party. High-end guest list, very private. And that was the last anyone saw of him. Housekeeper arrives twenty minutes ago, this is what she found." They see the balding man, now naked, an apple in his mouth and covered in blood. Catherine says faintly,

"Ex-chief of detectives." She then exposits in Brass' stead: "Left to make the big bucks. Consultant for security at every major casino in town and couldn't even protect himself." Gil thinks that the body's position and the fact that there is an apple in his mouth is a message. The message is: kill the pig. They learn that the wife is not at home, and neither is the daughter. Brass tells Catherine, "The housekeeper assumed she spent the weekend with her grandmother." Catherine dashes to the little girl's room, followed by Gil and Brass, and says that she's gone.

The other CSIs arrive and Gil informs them that the victim's wife, daughter, and Caddy are missing. They are to look for any signs of forced entry in the house, any signs of ransack that's not associated with the party. Sara's right on Grissom's heels, listening intently; Warrick and Nicky are not too far behind.

The coroner examines the body. The ex-chief was shot execution-style. The skin around his wrists is severely chafed by the handcuffs he's wearing, indicating that he tried to fight back. Meanwhile, Catherine's found a shell casing that seems to be standard police issue. They wonder aloud where the late ex-chief kept his gun.

They find the safe, and crime scene tech Scott drills his way into the safe. Catherine hands Brass assorted firearms as she finds them -- a .38, a pearl-handled .25 -- and a nice case containing a detective's badge, a brass plaque, and an empty spot where the gun should be.

Later in the driveway, Catherine theorizes that the wife did it. Gil rejects this—he says the wife would have planned better. The nanny told him she only took one shirt, one the kid wouldn't even wear. The two of them are interrupted when Lockwood approaches them with the estate security guard in tow. The guard doesn't have a list of party attendees, but he does have a record of every car that left. "Chief Rittle left at five AM...five-fourteen to be exact," the guard says, continuing that he was with his wife and kid, and he had his baseball cap and sunglasses on, like he always does. "So you saw a baseball cap and sunglasses. Did you actually see the chief's face?" Catherine clarifies. The guard isn't sure. He's saved by the bell when Catherine and Gil take off to check out the Caddy—Brass found it in a parking garage.

Catherine comes over and pops the trunk. There is a body in it. Apparently it stinks cause Brass gags and excuses himself, just in time to take a phone call. As he chats on the phone, Catherine pulls out a baseball cap, and she and Gil wonder about what his connection could be to the murder of the ex-chief. Brass is off the phone, and tells them "Florida Highway Patrol called. Several motorists saw a girl matching Sasha's exact physical description walking along an access road." Gil decides to send Catherine and Warrick to Miami to process.

Cut to Miami, at the site of a search party. Among the search party: Horation Caine. He dons his sunglasses and begins walking toward the lush greenery. He walks down a dirt road, stopping when he notices a faded pink plastic barrette in the road. He turns left, walking with a purpose, and eventually spots the little girl sitting with her back against the tree. He takes off his sunglasses and yells, "Sasha?" He walks towards her, and gently says: "My name is Horatio Caine. I'm head of the crime unit." Sasha asks about his name (he was named after Horatio Alger) and if Horatio's badge is real; Horatio hands it over and she says "My daddy's a policeman."

The next shot is of the Miami fuzz, gathered to look for a burgundy sedan with a thirty-two-year-old female and a male of indeterminate age. A helicopter whirrs above them and Catherine and Warrick. Horatio walks over to meet them and introduce himself.

Horatio tells them that social services has sent a doctor out; Catherine dons her Tough Cop mantle and says: "Let's just get one thing clear. This is a Las Vegas case, this is our victim, and we do the processing." Horatio says, "I didn't say he processed her, I just said he was here." Catherine calms a bit and puts on the mantle of politeness: "I appreciate the respect," she says. Warrick asks if Sasha's been told of her father's demise yet, and she hasn't. Caine directs Warrick to the trees and Catherine to the back of the ambulance where Sasha is sitting.

Catherine puts on the Mommy/Cop mantle and approaches Sasha. She asks, "Did the man touch you?' Sasha says that he hit her mom, but acted like she wasn't there. Catherine, meanwhile, has been trying to lift anything she can from Sasha's clothes, and then explains, "Well, you know what always happens to bad people? They leave behind a part of themselves, and that's how you can help us find your mommy. Now, I need to look under your fingernails." She takes Sasha's right hand, but the child's fingers are closed tightly around something—a shell casing. We flash back to Sasha being pushed out of the car by her mother and running off, her mother shouting frantically, "Run! Run! Run, Sasha, run!" We then see a gun firing. Switching from flashback cam to real-time cam, Sasha tells Catherine and Horatio, "I ran out after they drove off. I picked that up." Horatio says, "I bet it felt cold when you picked it up." Sasha says, "No, hot."

We cut immediately to a young woman who will later identify herself as Calleigh Buchanan holding the shell in question in the air, saying: "You can spot a Glock cartridge a block away. Rectangular firing pin impression, breach face sheer. This casing's no Glock. This isn't your chief's weapon." We are informed that that the shooter was a lousy shot. Catherine is clearly not taken with Calleigh. She asks:" You got a theory how the mother and daughter ended up in Miami from Las Vegas?" Catherine says: "We don't actually work theories, do we, Warrick?" Warrick backs her up and says "No, just evidence." Calleigh is able to laugh it off and says "We're much more fanciful down here. Aren't we, Horatio?...My guess is that this is a Taurus 9, made in Brazil. It's a cheap Baretta knock-off, and you may not see many of them in Vegas, but we get them down here all the time, which makes me think this guy wasn't fleeing Las Vegas."

Meanwhile, in the good old Vegas morgue, David and Gil are standing over the man that was found in the trunk. His name was Jason Doyle, dead for three days, which means he didn't shoot Rittle. David says he recovered one bullet from Doyle's cranium, and recovered a second fragment from Doyle's lower back. It was hanging out down there because the bullet entered his artery. The bullet used was from a 9MM, much like they found in the chief. Gil decides to share the news with Catherine.

At the mansion, Sara and Nicky are dusting the liquor bottles from the party. They get a hit on one of them: Tiffany Langer, a showgirl at the Orpheus Hotel. When they question her, she confirms that she was at the party, but she declines to confirm or deny anything else at this particular time. Apparently she has "worked hard" to get into whatever "circle" was at the party and doesn't wish to tarnish her reputation by ratting anyone out. She is happy, however, to rat out her date, as he wasn't in the Circle. Nicky asks if Tiffany knows where he is; Tiffany says, "I haven't seen him since that night. He sent me home with a judge and his wife." She tells them all she knows about him, which is not much, since she's only known him for five days. Apparently he is right-handed, a Libra, circumcised, old money Back East rich, and wore cheap cologne that smelled oddly sweet. This piques Gil's interest, and he finally coaxes Tiffany into coughing up his name: Adam Van der Welk.

In Florida, Catherine and Warrick explore the drop-off area. Warrick shouts that he's found a pill and Calleigh rushes over. It's a sedative, diazepam. Calleigh theorizes that the mother was force-fed diazepam and was ergo incapacitated; Horatio imagines the scenario, then wonders how the little girl got away. He has his own theory: the shooter pulled over the car to go to the bathroom, and while he was busy, the mother freed Sasha.

Turns out he's right—they walk a ways and find footprints leading to a rapidly drying puddle of urine. Catherine is thrilled, hoping some DNA loosed itself from the man's urethra while he was peeing. Just then, a cell phone rings. Horatio answers it, then says, "What do you mean, FBI?"

After a scenic montage of Miami scenery, we see Catherine on the phone with Gil, learning that the suspect may have had body odor, bad breath, or something else about him that made him smell. After Catherine gets off the phone, she meets Warrick and Calleigh, and learns that the FBI is involved cause the killer's profile matches someone they are after.

We establish that the FBI has no ID, but they have an M.O. -- the perp goes after wealthy couples. Speedle, a Miami CSI exposits that "Evidently the husbands get murdered, then the wives later -- after they've enjoyed forty-eight hours of fun and games."

Calleigh, Horatio, Catherine, and Warrick learn from the FBI that the car had been dumped at an estuary, and head there post haste. A Miami CSI named Delko dons scuba gear and gets in the water; a minute later, he surfaces and gives a thumbs-up, then a thumbs-down.

The next scene is of a crane pulling the vehicle out of the water. Horatio opens the door to the back seat. We see the body of a woman with duct tape over her mouth, wearing nothing but plastic rap. Catherine and Warrick give a positive ID. The body is taken to the morgue, where the coroner, Dr Woods, examines Mina Rittle's body: "Plastic's not for transport. Covering her intimates -- most likely sexual. Two gunshot wounds, left temple. One shot through and through...My preliminary probe shows water in the lungs, which indicates she was still alive when she was put in the canal...Looks like the eyes are glued shut. Gold, crusty substance underneath." Catherine guesses that the plastic was wrapped around Mina's eyes at some point, but came off underwater. Dr. Woods leans down to examine the victim's inner ear and discovers that it, too, is coated in the gold substance. In fact, the substance is in every orifice.

Back at the swampy estuary place, Speedle waits for Delko to surface. He does, with a water-logged Baretta knock-off.

Back in Las Vegas, Tiffany and the police sketch artist work together to get a picture of Adam. In Miami, Sasha's picture with the Miami sketch artist yields a sketch that matches the one in Vegas. Catherine wanders the CSI Miami office, pondering the fact that Tiffany saw a husband in Adam whereas Sasha had seen a monster.

Horatio emerges from a hallway and tells Catherine that the sticky gold substance they lifted off Mina was honey.

The next scene is of a bar, where women in bikinis made of saran wrap prance to and fro. A woman lies down in front of the bar, and two shirtless men pour honey on the women. The crowd then surges towards the woman with green apples, and dip it in the honey. Catherine realizes that this is where the killer got the idea. Horatio takes a swab of it.

In Las Vegas, Gil learns that Tuberculosis victims emit breath that smells like wet leaves. He is not convinced that the killer suffered from this particular ailment. Then the coroner tells him about diabetic ketoacidosis. The body has excess glucose which gets converted to ketone, which gets expelled through the pores, and has a fruity smell. Gil retrieves the baseball cap for testing.

At the lab in Miami, we learn that the sample is tupelo honey, the same kind of honey that was drizzled all over the late Mrs. Rittle. Warrick, the next day, goes to buy some tupelo honey and is shocked to find that a jar is $500. In another part of the building, Catherine shows the sketch to a bouncer and asks if he remembers Adam Van der Welk. He does not, but he does remember someone buying a whole carafe of the honey. It was the customer of a limo driver named Gordon.

In the next shot, Delko et al pull over a limo driver named Gordon Daimler. He is not thrilled with this development, as he is in a hurry to pick up a regular client of his with the last name Corwin. Catherine assures him that this won't take long, and asks about a customer of his that bought a jar of honey from the Hive. Gordon remembers this, but does not know the man's name because he paid in cash. Catherine asks, "Was there anything unusual about him? Did he smell? Did he have an odor?" Gordon raises an eyebrow, puzzled at the question, and said it smelled like he'd been drinking. Catherine wants to look in the limo, so Horatio jumps in the front and starts the car. A funny smell emits from the vents, one that Catherine describes as sickly sweet.

In Vegas, Grissom is making Tiffany smell the baseball cap and gets more information out of her: Adam only drank Dom.

The next scene is of Catherine is on the phone with Gil. She asks if it's possible to test for diabetic ketoacidosis off urine; Gil thinks that it might be. The medicine that one would take for such an ailment is called "Novolin insulin."

Not much later, the lab results of the urine are in, and
Catherine has a tech look through a database to find all the
people who take Novolin insulin, and have had to fulfill a
prescription in the last forty-eight hours. Gordon Daimler
is among them. Horatio theorizes that Gordon and Adam
are one and the same, and Gordon didn't smell because
he'd just taken his insulin. They look up Gordon's address.
They discover that the Corwins are currently the residents
of that address, which is a fancy waterfront property in a
high-rolling part of town, too expensive for a limo driver to
afford, that is. Catherine thinks Daimler uses the limo to
pick up his victims, and lives in their homes when they are
on vacation or at a second house.

Cut to a CSI car pulling into the Corwins' driveway. Horatio
leads the way, shouting "Miami-Dade Police!" They enter
and the teams split up -- Catherine and Horatio are paired,
and Warrick takes a back hall with Calleigh. In the
bedroom, Catherine throws back the bedcovers and finds
some plastic. Down in the basement, Warrick and Calleigh
find a pool of blood. Calleigh checks the pool of blood and
immediately says, "Nine-mil. Shots through and through.
Scalp hair. He fired this one first, to terrorize her." Warrick
looks at the second bullet hole and says, "This one here is
all business." Upstairs in the bathroom, Horatio has found
honey dripping down the tiles. He and Catherine decide
that she must have been assaulted on the bed, and then

dragged into the bathroom. They are interrupted Speedle comes in and says, "You guys gotta see this."

The thing that Speedle is so desperate to show them? The Corwins' dock is empty. Catherine decides that the killer has taken the boat and is off killing the Corwins on it as they speak. They call for reinforcement to search for the boat, and find it drifting offshore. About ten feet offshore, to be exact. Calleigh points out the figures on the infrared monitor. They are pink—this means that their body heat is fading. A red figure appears and the FBI guy says that it's the killer, and that the sniper should shoot. Calleigh disagrees—she thinks that the figure on the boat is helping the victims, not killing them. At that moment, Horatio remembers a picture of a plane in the Corwin's house. He thinks the killer is on the plane and the yacht is a diversion to buy time. Dennis and Horatio proceed to argue about who is in charge and what should be done; Dennis tells the sniper to shoot. Horatio tells him not to. He stands down. Horatio commands some of his colleagues to ground the plane and then he and Catherine sprint to the yacht. They open the door and find Mr. Corwin, sobbing and bloody, cries "I tried to save her. It was too late."

The next shot is of Gordon in the private jet, enjoying a bottle of Dom before fleeing the country. As Gordon lifts the glass to his lips, Horatio enters with his gun drawn. "

Gordon, pretty cool considering a gun is in his face, says "The Corwins are my friends. They lent me their plane...Speak to the pilot. Dylan Corwin called him personally, directed him to fly me to Monaco." Catherine informs him: "The husband didn't die. You left us a witness. We have enough evidence to convict you in two states." Gordon smiles and says, "Rich men don't go to jail." Horatio replies, "You're not rich, Gordon."

CSI Vegas bid CSI Miami goodbye. In the next scene, Horatio is charged with breaking the news to Sasha. " My mommy and daddy are dead, aren't they?" Horatio evasively answers "Well, your aunt is flying in to talk to you." She says "That's a yes." There's a quiet moment, and Horatio then says "Sasha, people are going to say things about your mom and dad, and some of them are going to be true. But what I want you to remember is that they fought like heroes for you. Will you remember that for me?" Sasha agrees to.

The Hunger Artist

The camera sweeps across the MGM Grand and the Luxor, and then switches to the interior of a lavish bathroom. A woman looks at a magazine while plucking her eyebrows, shown only from the back. The tub begins to overflow.

Gil is pulled from the lobby of a doctor's appointment for an unspecified ailment to arrive at a highway underpass somewhere in Vegas. We see Brass and Gil meet by a shopping cart to examine the unidentified body of a blonde woman, wrapped in a blanket and stuffed into a shopping car, her face marred by open sores. They are standing there not two minutes when a rat emerges from her mouth and runs off.

Gil paces around the scene, noticing a bloodstained rock under the bridge, and a red nylon Kate Spade purse, filled with syringes, tucked under the blanket.

At the morgue, however, we learn that her tox screen came up empty except for botulin. Gil and the corner look closely at the tiny, pinprick-like wounds in the dead woman's forehead, and tells him that they indicate repeated injections—probably of botox. However, in this case, whatever doctor treated her made a mistake. He or she missed the muscle and shot directly into her supratrochlear vein. David tells Gil that there are also possible signs of torture. The dovetail abrasion at the margins of the woman's cheek was caused the handle of a weapon scraping against her skin, meaning the blade was inserted more than once.

In another part of the lab, Sara examines the day planner found in the Kate Spade bag next to the needles. The entry at top reads in the "+" column "T3 C 1023," and in the "-" column "-10 OK, =0." Warrick stops by and takes a look commenting that it could be the sort of scribble that speed freaks dabble in when they've been up all night.

Meanwhile, Dusty the photo artist works magic on a photo of the woman's scarred face. She airbrushes and uses other Photoshop secrets to even out her skin, and give her perfectly manicured brows. A beautiful face with flawless bone structure emerges from the screen. Dusty looks the image after giving her blonde hair and blue eyes and says, "I know her from somewhere."

Where does she know her from? The cover of the 2001 issue of Showbiz Weekly. Her name, as it turns out, is Ashleigh. Gil picks up the autopsy photo and compares it to the magazine cover. Catherine concludes that someone wanted her dead. He also concludes that someone wanted her ugly.

In the next scene, Gil, Catherine, and brass enter Ashleigh's urban loft style apartment in a gentrified neighborhood of Vegas. She has decorated it with a lot of professional-quality photos of herself, including three posters. Gil notices a small pile of minty-smelling white powder on a side table. Since the tox screen was clean, Catherine opines that a boyfriend may have been the user. Brass, Nicky, and Warrick check the inside of the victim's car and find that it's littered with junk food wrappers, and more magazines that feature her as the cover model. They also find a hand-written note that reads:

"Babe -- he's not good enough for you. He doesn't have the history we do. You mean the world to me. I know you'll live to regret this decision."

In the bathroom, Catherine notes blood in the sink, but none on the floor, then finds a Costco-style pallet of enemas. Gil digs in the trash and then pulls out a bag filled with a something that looks like blood. He finds a bloody handprint on the wall, and in the closet, Catherine notices an old coat with a piece of coral-colored scarf on the floor. The shoulder is ripped. In the kitchen, Gil opens a drawer and sees a pile of syringes and in the fridge is nothing but sweet and low and botox jars. It seems as though Ashleigh was giving herself Botox injections.

Gil, deep in thought, wanders off and walks to the crime scene. Sara's there, making sure she missed nothing when she went over the shopping cart and the purse in the lab. They decide she must have been pushed to the underpass in a shopping cart. They then notice in a Eureka moment that the cart—and Ashleigh's body—was parked under a billboard welcoming people to Las Vegas. Ashleigh is at the helm of the welcome wagon.

Back at the lab, they examine the cart again. Ashleigh's body was stuffed in the cart along with newspapers, Las Vegas Review-Journals, the Sun, a couple of tennis rackets, a broom, an umbrella, a pot, and a glove. All of the papers and journals and magazines have at least one picture of Ashleigh in it.

Out on the street, Nicky and Warrick knock at the apartment inhabited by the author of the note they found in the car. The author is not in. He has, however, left his trash on the sidewalk for collection, which means they don't need a warrant. Warrick finds a brown paper bag containing a torn of photo of the victim.

The next scene is of a photo shoot taking place in Venice. (The casino. Not the Italian city). The agent screams at a model gaining weight, calling her a cow, and she runs off in tears.

He is interrupted by Catherine and Brass. They introduce themselves, and he says: "Sorry about Ashleigh. She wasn't a client anymore. I dropped her a couple of months ago...She was a screwed-up kid, looking for a father figure. One minute I'm booking a photo shoot, the next minute, she's screaming for Daddy." A man not too far away hears this and charges Rod, trying to stab him with tableware from a local café. Brass separates them, and the next scene is of the man in the interrogation tank.

He says, "Rod did everything he could to make her totally dependent on him." Warrick asks if Ashleigh left him for Rod, and if so, is this was prompted him to tear up a picture of her? Rod responds: "If you were in love with an amazing woman, and you knew she was throwing away everything amazing about her on some scum...would you still want her picture on your desk?" he asks. "Well, no, because my love is highly conditional," replies Brass, continuing, "What'd you use to cut up the picture? The same knife you used on Rod? The same knife you used to cut up Ashleigh's face?" The man looks stunned.

CSI Las Vegas: Season Two

Rod, by the way, was dragged into the tank as well. He denies sleeping with her though he admits that his things were in her apartment because as her agent, he had a duty to "protect his asset!" Rod clarifies, "She needed constant attention, supervision. Leave her alone for a minute, fill in the blank." Catherine is left speechless.

Meanwhile, Sara is examining the coat that Catherine found crumpled up on the floor of Ashleigh's closet. The coat has crabs. She invites him to peer into the microscope and look, and he does, and says: "We have a high-end handbag found in a street person's shopping cart, a jacket covered in crabs in a closet full of designer clothes -- what does that tell us?" Sara thinks that Ashleigh had a homeless guest; Gil thinks that whoever is missing his shopping cart is also missing a jacket.

Inspired, Gil returns to an alley near Ashleigh's loft. He sees a homeless man with a bloodstained scarf digging through a garbage can and immediately offers to trade his jacket for the scarf. The man agrees and wanders off. A homeless woman who saw all this go down approaches Gil and he sees the expensive ring the woman is wearing. He immediately volunteers to trade his Maglite for her ring and for the leather grooming case has, which, incidentally, looks just like one that Ashleigh had in her loft. The woman agrees and as she turns over the ring, we see a speck of something dart across her hand.

He takes the items back to the lab and we learn that the blood on the scarf matches Ashleigh's but the blood on the murder weapon matches Rod's. The epithelials on the ring, however, belong to someone related to Ashleigh.

Gil returns to the same alley in hopes of finding the woman he got the ring from, and he finds her. He makes small talk with her, and buys her a hot dog. She seems somewhat mentally imbalanced, going on and on about the importance of a healthy and low calorie diet. Eventually Gil asks, "How about your sister?" She stammers, "My-my sister didn't have a sister." She then explains more about dieting and the importance of staying away from carbs etc. Gil listens and then asks about the scarf he traded his jacket for. "He says, "Did your sister give that to you? Or did you steal it from her?" Cassie says contemptuously, "I should have stole it. Because she-she stole from me." Gil asks, "What did she steal from you?" "My life," Cassie says.

The next scene takes place at the modeling agency, where Rod is explaining that he washed his hands of Cassie, explaining that "for every piece of meat, there has to be a butcher." Catherine suggests that perhaps Rod led Cassie to the slaughter; Rod shows the CSIs to a blow-up of a Spa

World magazine, with a January 2000 cover. The cover girl is Cassie. Rod gestures at it and says," See, Cassie got deep into freebase. No shortage of scumbags around to keep her supplied. I knew she had the sister in Wichita Falls..." In flashback cam, we see one of Cassie's last photo shoots, where her mood swings far and wide between heroin-induced lethargy and coke-fueled fury. Rod sighs an turns to look at Ashleigh, looking less like a supermodel and more like the girl next door, and decides that Ashleigh is a far better investment. Rod continues with this story in real time, saying "Cassie was an obsessed base head. Cocaine already had her paranoid. Once Ashleigh started modeling, everything became this big conspiracy. Naturally, yours truly was Satan." Gil summarizes the whole thing by saying "Cassie threw her life away and her sister Ashleigh recycled it."

Back at the lab, Sara's still tries to figure out the code in Ashleigh's day planner. So far, based on the details she has about Ashleigh, she thinks that "BFJ3" means BF, or Bellagio Fountain." 3J = J. J. Jarrett, a famous photographer. Sara also notes that Ashleigh stopped working as a model two months ago.

In the interrogation tank, Brass confronts Cassie and tries to get her to admit to killing her sister. Cassie makes some sense as she babbles: "I tried to warn her, the in-ing and the out-ing and the pick-pick, and the counting, and the counting, and the counting. I mean, I did, I tried. That's why I tried to really really save her...She could never be pretty enough, and she could never be skinny enough, and she could never be perfect enough, and she could never be anything enough."

Then we go into flashback cam. We see Ashleigh at a shoot, in tears, and Rod telling her" Hey, fat girl. I got what you need," before giving her cocaine. In another scene, we see interchanging images of Rod yelling at Ashleigh; then Cassie, then Ashleigh, then back to Cassie, over and over. Then a flash of Ashleigh vomiting, then more flashes between both girls looking sad and emaciated.

Brass interrupts and says "She's a needle freak, she doesn't know what she's talking about." Gil shushes him and asks Cassie if she tried to stop and couldn't. Cassie flies across the table at him. She is subdued by the uniforms, and taken to a holding cell.

Deep in thought, Gil goes to the morgue and as he walks in, the coroner says "I found blisters in the back of her throat...and worn enamel on the tooth in conjunction with this red mark on the knuckle of her middle finger....She was bulimic -- and anorexic, which explains the down on her skin. Lanugo."

Anyway the coroner continues, saying that this did weaken the immune system, but the cause of death was a failed kidney fueled by septicemia. Add that to other symptoms -- anemia, a low red blood cell count, low iron, and high ESR—and in Gil's words, "She didn't just die. She's been dying for a long time."

Gil then retreats to his office and is joined moments later by Catherine, who has Cassie James's psych profile. Cassie's apparently a classic paranoid schizophrenic. Maybe Ashleigh was, and that's what explains the picking at her face? They then establish that Cassie's prints place her in her sister's apartment.

Meanwhile, Sara is going through all the wrappers found in the car. She sorts through everything and a light bulb goes on. She cracks the day planner code using nutrition labels as the key. Meanwhile, Greg tells Warrick that the skin found under Ashleigh's fingernails was her own.

Sara, in the next scene, is explaining the code: Bulimia is a zero sum disorder. Whatever went in had to be exactly cancelled by what went out." Sara theorizes that she had body dysmorphic disorder, and goes on to explain what it is. "One theory suggests it's neurological, another that it's neurobiological, another that it's psychological -- people with extreme sexual or emotional anxiety unconsciously displace their feelings into the arena of appearance because it's more manageable." The gouges in Ashleigh's face? "Meticulous grooming when a person suffers from BDD becomes a destructive compulsion. One line that keeps repeating again in her daybook, over and over and over again -- 'I'm not even...A large number of BDD sufferers are convinced that they're not symmetric, that one side of their face doesn't match the other.... The bottom line is...control and perfectionism. That's what her code was all about. Let's take HBWC/3 1590 BC 90 BF 3930 S 114 TC. Three hamburgers with cheese, calories 530, five-thirty times three is where she gets 1590 BC. That's BC for bad calories, and at 30 grams a pop, that's 90 grams of BF...[bad fat]. The rest of her formula involves sodium, total carbohydrates, and the actual weight of everything she ate."

Gil says, "So she was operating like a scientist, seeking the perfect formula to take her pain away." Sara responds, "Or disappears all together. Which brings me to the minus side of the equation. She would write down the number of times she TU'd -- threw up, in this case, twice – or [moved her bowels]. The directions on her disposable enema box use the term 'evacuate,' so after her burger binge, she 3 EVO'd 14 G, 2 TU'd 9 G and 3 #1. She evo'd three times, but her calculations didn't stop there. G stands for grams." We get a view in flashback cam of Ashleigh weighing her feces in plastic bags.

Gil sums it all up. "She attacked herself. Ashleigh was convinced that everything about her needed to be fixed. The real problem was inside her head -- that's why she tried to fix the outside." We are taken to flashback cam, where see Ashleigh sitting down before the mirror, digging and jabbing into her skin over and over. Gil wraps it up with, "So the victim and the killer became one and the same. The very nature of addiction, whether it be self-medicating or self-mutilating, is that the behavior we use to survive it becomes the behavior that ends up killing us." OK fine but how did she end up in a shopping cart with a rat in her mouth, under a freeway overpass? We go again to flashback cam. We see Ashleigh stumble across her loft after digging around in her face, and come to collapse on her bed. We then see Cassie silently looking down at her sister, rocking back and then washing her hands so she can drag Ashleigh off the bed. Gil opines that Cassie was trying to take care of her sister. She pushed her to a place where she thought she'd be safe. Where she thought she could see herself for how beautiful she really was. Again we flash back, this time to Cassie wheeling Ashleigh, who is either unconscious or dead—it's not clear-- so she would have been able to see the billboard of herself if her eyes had been open.

In the next scene, Gil walks Cassie to the neighborhood in which he found her, and gives her a new shopping cart. He asks if she'd like help getting into a shelter, and she says no. She says she'd need shelter from a shelter. He watches her walk off.

We then Gil standing on a crowded sidewalk but the sounds of the street go in and out. . Gil walks over to a fountain tries to hear if the sound of the fountain changes according to how close he is too it. He's so engrossed in this that he almost gets hit by a car he didn't hear barreling towards him. Everything gets muffled. Then we hear a voice-over of him: "Obviously, most of crime-scene investigation is about seeing, but much of it is about hearing as well. Listening. Knowing how to listen. Not just to what people are saying, but how they say it. How their tone of voice matches their facial expressions or body posture. So even if I read lips and know what they're saying, it's not enough."

Then we find him at a doctor's office and learn he has otosclerosis, the auditory impairment that caused his mother's deafness. He asks how long it will take for him to lose his hearing completely. She says she doesn't know. "How long, do you think?" "I don't know," she replies, thus leaving impending deafness dangling over the series' head until the end of the summer break.

INDEX

www.ingramcontent.com/pod-product-compliance
Lightning Source LLC
Chambersburg PA
CBHW031946090426
42739CB00006B/107